HOW TO SUCCEED IN YOUR HOME BUSINESS

BEATING THE BIGGIES WITH BETTER QUALITY

LARRY EASTO

HOME BUSINESS PRESS
WILLOWDALE, ONTARIO
CANADA

Published by

Home Business Press
281 Poyntz Avenue
Willowdale, Ontario
M2N 1J8

CANADIAN CATALOGUING IN PUBLICATION DATA

Easto, Larry, 1944 -

   How to succeed in your home business

Includes bibliographical references and index.
ISBN 0-9696967-0-1

1. Home-based businesses. I. Title

HD2333.E3 1993   658'.041   C93-93678-7

Cover Design: Greg Salmela
Interior Design and Typesetting: Joanne Kennedy

Table of Contents

ABOUT THE AUTHOR

Larry Easto, certified a Professional Consultant by the Academy of Professional Advisors and Consultants, has been actively involved with small business for more than 20 years. He has operated his consulting practice from his home for the past 8 years.

Trained and qualified as a lawyer, he practised law for more than 12 years, working primarily in the area of business law. During this period, he worked with clients in all aspects of their businesses operations: from purchase to sale, from start-up to wind-up. As a practising lawyer, Mr. Easto believed that legal services should be oriented to problem prevention rather than problem resolution. *"Too much time, energy and money is devoted to trying to make the best of a bad situation — trying to put Humpty Dumpty back together again. These resources would be better used trying to find Humpty Dumpty a better, and safer, place to sit."*

As a result of the orientation towards prevention, client education was a major component of his legal services. Mr. Easto also taught a variety of business and law courses and wrote articles for a wide range of publications.

Shifting from law to consulting, he provided services in the areas of strategic planning, marketing and human resource training and development. These service areas provided a more structured and focused approach to the practice of problem prevention. *"Strategic planning is the process of deciding where you want to go and how you want to get there. It sets a direction that makes it possible for you to achieve your goals while minimizing the risks."*

While associated with Ernst & Young as Manager, National Entrepreneurial Services, the author was introduced to Total Quality Management or TQM. *"I was intrigued by two aspects of TQM. First, the idea of doing it right the first time was essentially problem prevention. Second, the underlying principles and concepts of quality management and quality service, reflected the intuitive activities of successful small business people."* Since these principles are so compatible with his own experience, they have formed an important part of his work on increasing profits with improved quality, including the design and delivery of a number of quality improvement workshops.

Working from his home, Larry has designed and led many planning retreats and assisted a number of small businesses with the development and implementation of marketing plans. His training activities include both standard management programs and programs specially designed to meet the needs of individual clients. He has spoken widely at continuing education seminars and workshops; his articles have appeared in local, regional and national publications.

Larry now continues his consulting practice exclusively from his home office. He shares his office with his family, who use the computer for school projects, and a dog who uses the computer desk as a refuge from thunderstorms.

S.W.

ACKNOWLEDGEMENTS

This book exists because a number of people did what they said they were going to do. In most cases, they exceeded expectations.

My family experienced first hand what it's like to write a book. As well as loads of patience and understanding, my wife Connie was a superb editor, continuing to find opportunities to improve the material — even when I was satisfied. Megan and Hayley, our daughters, provided two essential ingredients: space and support.

My parents and my brother Bob and his wife Louise all contributed necessary support at a critical time; Don and Fran were a welcome addition to the team as the project progressed.

Don Fraser, Jaime Watt, and Bob Langmuir all read an early draft. Each found a variety of mistakes and offered suggestions as to better form and readability.

Greg Salmela and the rest of the creative people at Thomas Watt Cohen & McCall pooled their talents to produce the right cover with the right components. Chris Walker, also of Thomas Watt, in co-ordinating his firm's work on the book, continued to demonstrate quality client service on an ongoing basis.

Very early in the writing process, I abandoned a state of the art wordprocessing program in favour of a more standard one with which I was more comfortable. Joanne Kennedy did the same in typesetting the material. With the help of, and often in spite of, the variety of interesting and talented people who continue to flow in and around Cameron Kennedy & Associates Ltd., Joanne demonstrated that artistry is the difference between simple typesetting (aka Desktop Publishing) and creative typography.

All of these people helped turn a large and sometimes lonely project into a group effort to produce the book you hold.

Thanks to each and every one of you. This book would not have been possible without your unique contribution.

Larry Easto
Willowdale, Ontario
March, 1993

PREFACE

For the remainder of this decade, home businesses will continue to thrive in an increasingly competitive economy. Requiring lower overhead costs, they can be extremely profitable; operating with fewer structural and bureaucratic constraints, they can provide better and faster client service. Because they reflect the personal goals, and indeed the personality, of the individual operating the business, there is virtually no limit to job satisfaction. Our current information age has made home based businesses more viable and attractive than ever before.

Home businesses can compete effectively with their larger counterparts. They can, in fact, gain a competitive edge over larger and more traditional business organizations by using the principles of quality client service. Although many large business organizations have adopted so-called quality management programs, home based businesses are better able to deliver quality client service. **How to Succeed in Your Home Business** will show how.

In showing how to deliver quality service, the book identifies and discusses ten basic truths about client service. These basic truths are important to all business and service organizations, regardless of size. They can serve as an ongoing reference as to what client service is all about. The book also clarifies what clients are really looking for and how you can respond to these client needs and expectations. Like the truths, these factors apply to all business organizations. Indeed these same principles apply to the service component of all businesses regardless of whether they supply products or services. Although they appear to be basic and common sense issues, many businesses forget about them, especially when they are operating in survival mode.

Realistically, "going out on your own", "running your own business" or "being your own boss" is not the right approach for everyone. If you have any doubts as to whether or not to start your own home business, the assessment found in the Introduction will give you some insight into how you are likely to fare as an entrepreneur. If the assessment leads you to conclude that running a home business is not your cup of tea, don't despair; not everyone has the combination of personal skills, attitude and resources to take on such a project. There are many other options for you to explore.

If you decide that a home business might be a realistic goal for you, this book will help. You will learn what's right about home businesses and why they will continue to thrive in the future. You will also learn, in a very practical way, what you need to start your own business. A start-up checklist will help you identify the specifics of what you need to start your business.

If you currently operate your own home business you will learn how to market it. The chapter on measuring client satisfaction will enable you to learn how satisfied your clients are. This will help you to maintain, or preferably improve, the level of your current client's satisfaction and to develop new marketing initiatives.

Although you can successfully operate your home business alone, you should involve as many others as possible. Among other benefits, you will enjoy being able to draw on a broader range of services to provide to your clients. Through networking, you can replace for yourself the personal contact that can otherwise be lost through working at home.

For small businesses, home based formats can be very profitable and attractive. Employing the same principles used by larger business organizations, home business operations can gain and maintain a competitive edge over their larger counterparts.

HOW TO USE THE BOOK

The following table will help you to quickly find material that is most relevant to you and your current situation. You may wish to read those sections first.

BROWSERS' QUICK REFERENCE GUIDE

How do I...	See...
...know whether I can and should run a home business?	..entrepreneurial assessment in the introduction
...select a business that I can operate at home?	...chapters 2-3 and books listed in Appendix B
...start a home business?	...chapters 12-14
...showcase my home business?	...Appendix A
...market my services, regardless of the size of my business?	...chapters 15-16
...improve the quality of client service, regardless of the size of my business?	...chapter 8-11
...measure client' satisfaction?	...chapter 17
...involve others in my business?	...chapter 18
...locate associations to join?	...Appendix A
...find a specific topic in the book?	...index
...locate other books and publications	...Appendix B

INTRODUCTION

HOW ENTREPRENEURIAL ARE YOU?

Operating any business from home requires more than having a quality product or service. It requires a broad range of entrepreneurial skills and attitudes.

The following assessment, although not scientifically tested, will provide some insight as to your entrepreneurial orientation. Psychologists, successful entrepreneurs and consultants believe these attitudes and behaviourial patterns are related to you ultimate success as an entrepreneur. Scoring instructions and suggestions as to possible interpretations follow the assessment.

As with any self-assessment, your final score and rating are not as important as the consideration that you give to the issues raised as you complete the exercise. You may be required to think about questions and concepts that are new to you. If this happens, address the issue as thoroughly as you can. Entrepreneurs, especially those operating home businesses, do not always have the luxury of ducking issues by referring them to some one else for resolution.

ENTREPRENEURIAL ASSESSMENT

The following questions deal with your personal background, behaviourial characteristics and lifestyle patterns.

Answer the questions by marking the response that most accurately reflects your attitude. Answer every question as honestly as you can.

Part I: Attitudes Toward Risk Taking

	Definitely Yes	Probably Yes	Probably No	Definitely No
1. I am prepared to make sacrifices in my family life and to take a cut in pay to succeed in my own business.	☐	☐	☐	☐
2. I take risks for the thrill of it.	☐	☐	☐	☐
3. I enjoy doing something just to prove that I can.	☐	☐	☐	☐
4. I enjoy tackling a task without knowing all the potential problems.	☐	☐	☐	☐

Part II: Personal Initiative and Discipline

	Definitely Yes	Probably Yes	Probably No	Definitely No
5. Once I decide to do something, I will do it and nothing can stop me.	☐	☐	☐	☐
6. When I begin a task, I set clear goals and objectives for myself.	☐	☐	☐	☐
7. After a severe setback in a project, I am able to pick up the pieces and start over again.	☐	☐	☐	☐
8. I am usually able to come up with more than one way to solve a problem.	☐	☐	☐	☐
9. I believe in organizing my tasks before getting started.	☐	☐	☐	☐
10. I find myself constantly thinking up new ideas.	☐	☐	☐	☐
11. I can concentrate on one subject for extended periods of time.	☐	☐	☐	☐
12. I find unexpected energy resources as I tackle things I like.	☐	☐	☐	☐
13. I am likely to work long hours to accomplish a goal.	☐	☐	☐	☐

Part III: General Attitudes

	Definitely Yes	Probably Yes	Probably No	Definitely No
14. When I do a good job, I am satisfied in knowing personally that the job has been well done.	☐	☐	☐	☐
15. I like the feeling of being in charge.	☐	☐	☐	☐
16. When I think of the future, I envision my self running my own business.	☐	☐	☐	☐
17. I try to do a better job than is expected of me.	☐	☐	☐	☐
18. Personal satisfaction means more to me than having money to spend on myself.	☐	☐	☐	☐
19. I try to find the benefits in a bad situation.	☐	☐	☐	☐
20. I persist when others tell me it can't be done.	☐	☐	☐	☐
21. I enjoy being able to make my own decisions on the job.	☐	☐	☐	☐
22. I can accept failure without admitting defeat.	☐	☐	☐	☐
23. I strive to use past mistakes as learning processes.	☐	☐	☐	☐
24. I find that answers to problems come out of nowhere.	☐	☐	☐	☐
25. I prefer to make final decisions on my own.	☐	☐	☐	☐

Scoring:

The above questions all reflect traditional entrepreneurial attitudes. Scoring for these questions is:

4 points for each question answered "Definitely yes"
3 points for each question answered "Probably yes"
2 points for each question answered "Probably no"
1 point for each question answered "Definitely no".

Interpretation:

Total Score

above 75 Definitely Entrepreneurial

Your combination of personal background and behaviour and lifestyle patterns should give you the basis for a successful business.

50 - 74 Possibly Entrepreneurial

You might have the basis for a successful business. The assessments involved in preparing your business plan can serve as a second opinion as to whether or you should proceed with the development of your own business.

26 - 49 Probably Not Entrepreneurial

Other possibilities may be more suitable to your personality and attitudes. There are many resources such as *What Color Is Your Parachute?* listed in Appendix C.

under 25 Definitely Not Entrepreneurial

This is self explanatory; you will probably work best as an employee.

It is prudent to bear in mind that many people, because of their temperament attitudes, life circumstances and past experiences are more likely to be happy and productive as employees than as entrepreneurs.

1 THE GROWTH OF HOME BUSINESS

Our society is changing more dramatically and more rapidly than at any other time in history. At one time it was thought that the harder you worked, the better off you would be. We now know that hard work does not always lead to personal and economic success. Nor is it good for the body: the stress-related consequences of working too hard are well known.

Millions of people are learning that bigger is not necessarily better. Mass layoffs at seemingly invincible giants like General Motors suggest that long term security in large organizations is more myth than reality. Cutbacks and contracting out of services have resulted in the loss of millions of jobs in North America.

Fortunately, there is light on the economic horizon. Home businesses will continue to thrive in an increasingly competitive marketplace.

Millions of entrepreneurs already enjoy running their own businesses from home. Over the next few years, millions more will join their ranks. There are many reasons for this growth.

Following are some of these reasons:

Beating Stress

Individually and collectively, we know more about stress and stress management than any other generation in history. Hardly a week goes by without some authority telling us that we should watch our diets, exercise more, smoke and drink less and generally improve the manner in which we manage our work and home lives. We are exposed to enough information on the subject that we should by now all be experts on the subject of "burnout".

Although acutely aware of the negative impact of too much work, many individuals are driven by the desire for more money or more status. They work more rather than fewer hours. Like shooting stars, they are on the rise; like shooting stars they will sooner or later burn themselves out.

Fortunately, an increasing number of people are accepting the validity of the ongoing stress advisories and are committed to beating burnout. For many of these people, operating businesses from their homes helps to eliminate a large volume of work related stress.

Commuting and its broad range of associated hassles becomes a non-issue. Questions such as why there is never a bus when you need one or why today's trendy cologne and last night's garlic dinner produce such a vile combination on the crowded subway can be left to others to ponder. Similarly, it no longer matters what that crazy driver is trying to do in zig-zagging across three lanes of commuter traffic. Best of all, the hours that would otherwise have been spent commuting can be put to other uses.

Workers whose jobs involve working on computers and talking on telephones are finding that their working time is more productive and less stressful when performed in home offices. At a time when many people simply talk about changing their lifestyles to improve the quality of their lives, those who work at home are actually doing it. The shift from busy, often sterile, climate controlled office premises to a more subdued home environment eliminates most of the work-a-day stressors: noise, crowding and unwelcome interruptions. With less time required for commuting, there is more time for family and personal interests. The desire to minimize stress and improve the quality of life will serve to encourage the trend to home businesses.

Breaking Barriers

Pay equity legislation has been designed to ensure that workers receive equal compensation for work of equal value. The fact that such legislation is necessary serves to emphasize the reality that barriers to fair and equitable compensation and to career advancement do exist. These barriers may be based on gender (commonly referred to as "The Glass Ceiling") race, age, nationality or some other factor.

Established business organizations tend to be rigidly structured. Acceptance of these structures and the rigidity that accompanies them are seen as the price to be paid for the organization's stability and longevity. Unfortunately the structures severely limit career advancement and pay increases for many people. Running a home business can represent a realistic and viable alternative.

Cashing In

Not too many years ago, it was often true that an employee who worked hard and did everything that the employer asked would be looked after up to and beyond retirement. Attractive as this situation may have been for many people, it is no longer common. Employees in all sectors of the economy are beginning to realize that fewer people retire from large business organizations after many years of devoted service. As the ranks of middle management continue to be savagely reduced, formerly loyal employees are reviewing their own prospects for continuous future employment.

Clearly, the dismissal of yet another employee with more than 25 years service forces many individuals to seriously consider their own options. As they do so, they see their organizations in a new light. They see organizations that are no longer prepared to protect their employees as if they were children. As large business organizations become leaner and meaner, employees see themselves simply as means to an end: an end that is less humane and more bottom line oriented.

Not surprisingly, after considering the whole picture, many of these employees decide they neither need nor want the discomfort and uncertainty that are new features of the once enjoyable job. Like a player ready to leave a poker game, they would like to cash in the career chips that they have been stacking up over the years and leave the firm to go somewhere else to work at what they really want to do.

It doesn't take long for them to realize that there simply are not enough existing jobs to go around. For some, self-employment becomes a very realistic and viable way to replace the uncertainties of working for a large and impersonal organization. For many, self employment often starts with a home business.

Contracting Out

In difficult economic times, all organizations must actively seek cost saving opportunities. Contracting out services has become a very common strategy. In essence, contracting out involves purchasing from outside sources specific services that were formerly performed internally by employees of the organization.

Putting aside the concerns of organized labour, contracting out represents a win-win strategy for both the purchaser and the supplier of the services. The purchaser pays only for those services that are actually used.

Take, for example, the contracting out of computer programming services. Instead of paying the salary, benefits and overhead costs of maintaining full time computer programming capability, the purchaser would pay only the cost of contracted computer programming, as these costs are incurred. Although the hourly cost may well be higher than the corresponding hourly cost if performed by employees, the total annual cost could be substantially lower. Ideally, the purchaser receives the same volume of services at a lower overall cost.

In providing services by contract, the computer programmer becomes an independent contractor and will realize certain tax advantages as a result of this status. These advantages include the ability to deduct specific expenses from business income in calculating income tax. To be deductible, the expenses must have been incurred for the purpose of generating business income.

Further, as an independent contactor, the programmer could

also provide services to a number of purchasers. This can result in a significantly higher income potential than would be possible as an employee. Thus the programmer could provide more services to more clients and generate a higher overall income.

As contracting out becomes more commonly used, the range of services required becomes increasingly broader. This in turn will continue to increase the potential for home business.

Computer Technology

There is no question that the current growth in home business is largely driven by advances in computer technology. Individuals who work with knowledge and with information require computers and associated telecommunications equipment to perform their tasks. They need little in terms of office premises or support staff. Those secretarial and other services that they do require can be purchased as needed on a fee for service basis.

Increasingly, people who work primarily on computers are finding that they usually work as well, if not better, from home than they do from organizational offices. This growth of home entrepreneurs is new and unprecedented. It is a trend that will continue to grow over the next decade.

Cutting Back

If pay equity is one of the hottest human resource issues of the decade, excess capacity must be the most widespread economic issue. There are simply too many suppliers of goods and services chasing too few customers.

The most prevalent means of dealing with this excess capacity is to cut back in every area possible. Unfortunately, virtually all cutbacks ultimately result in the termination of employees' jobs. Regardless of what the termination is called — lay off, let go, dismissal, rightsizing or early retirement — the end result is the same: employees lose their jobs and are out of work.

Like the employees who have cashed in their career chips and voluntarily left their employment, it doesn't take long for terminated employees to realize that there are not enough jobs to go around. Also like those who chose to leave their jobs, those who leave involuntarily can consider self-employment in a home business as a realistic and viable option.

Once established and settled into running their own businesses, many of these people begin to see their terminations as blessings in disguise. Looking back, their previous jobs do not appear as great as they thought at one time. No longer having to follow the party line, they are free to recognize and admit the frustrations that formed part of the fabric of their jobs and the overall work environment. Many realize that much of their time and energy on the job was directed to following established patterns and maintaining the status quo. The challenge of personal growth and development, once an important driving force, had been replaced by the burden keeping the organizational machinery moving.

Operating their own home business, many people experience a sense of renewal. They have a renewed sense of energy and commitment to their jobs and to their clients. Instead of seeing their terminations as crises, they recognize the end of their jobs as opportunities for new growth and development. For them and for many, home businesses represent the potential for new and exciting possibilities.

2 BUSINESSES THAT CAN BE OPERATED FROM THE HOME

The first home businesses, in fact the first independent businesses, were operated by skilled tradesmen and artisans. Goods of all kinds — primarily to meet the personal and household needs and those of agriculture and defence — were produced from the homes of the craftsmen and sold directly to the end users. With the coming of the Industrial Revolution, enterprising individuals realized that by bringing these workers together in a common workplace, more goods could be produced at a lower per unit cost. Eventually, Henry Ford developed his assembly line and the principles of mass production became the operative business practice for most of the twentieth century.

Now, as the Industrial Age loses its momentum, we are experiencing a resurgence of interest in home businesses. Today's broad range of business activities and opportunities provides an equally broad range of choices for the home business entrepreneur. The best choices require a minimum of space and equipment and focus primarily on the personal skills and ability of the business operator.

Supplying Products

Manufactured By You

Most manufacturing operations require too much capital or are too labour intensive to be viable home business operations. Economic considerations apart, few of us would voluntarily turn our homes into factories. Production operations involving any or all of high volume, sophisticated production operations and a large work force are best left to large industrial organizations.

The production of unique specialty items, on the other hand, is ideally suited to home business operation. This would include such traditional artisan type businesses as dressmaking, jewellery making, pottery and woodworking. In each of these businesses, the emphasis should be on the uniqueness and the quality of the work produced. With effective marketing strategies, producers of unique, high quality goods will continue to be successful. Conversely, I really doubt that the world needs yet another lawn ornament made from recycled bleach bottles.

Manufactured By Others

Many successful home businesses involve the distribution of products manufactured by others. Typical businesses fit into the distribution chain anywhere from purchasing directly from the manufacturer to purchasing from sub-distributors and selling to the ultimate consumer. Examples of these businesses include distributing cosmetics, jewellery, cleaning supplies and a great variety of other products regardless of when and where they were manufactured.

Distributing the products of others can be done through a variety of operating formats. Wholesalers, distributors and retailers purchase goods for resale. Their income is generated by selling goods at a higher price than they paid for them. These people must pay for the goods they purchase for resale, regardless of whether or not they succeed in selling them.

Franchises are common methods of distributing goods. They have been described as the most successful marketing concept ever created. A franchise organization is in fact a contractual association between a franchisor (the manufacturer or wholesaler) and independent franchisees who purchase the right to distribute the franchisor's products. There are approximately 500,000 franchised business operations in the U.S.A. and Canada with a new franchise opening every 8 minutes.

An estimated 4,500 franchisors provide a broad range of franchise opportunities. Many of the opportunities represent great potential for home business operators. Suitable service areas include: beauty and health, business, computer, education, maintenance, photography and publicity. Dozens of directories and handbooks are available in public libraries and book stores to detail various franchise opportunities. These resources also outline what to look for and what to avoid in purchasing a franchise.

Another growing trend is the use of multi-level marketing. As the name suggests, this involves a number of different levels of distributors. The manufacturer sells products to a high level distributor who in turn resells the products to the next lower level of distributor. This lower level sells to yet a lower level and so on. The purchasing and reselling continues until ultimately the products are sold to the end user. Programs used by such companies as Amway, Mary Kaye Cosmetics and Tupperware are typical multi-level marketing arrangements. Contemporary advancements in communications technology and services such as overnight delivery from factory to home, increase the attractiveness and profitability of these businesses. As is the case with franchises, there are a number of resources available to provide guidance with respect to these business opportunities.

Another approach to distribution, also suitable for home business, is the use of sales or manufacturers' representatives or agents. These people never actually own products supplied by others. They take orders for the manufacturer or supplier, who pays them a commission. Unless otherwise agreed, commissions are payable when the supplier receives payment for the goods sold.

Growing nostalgia has given new life to the expression that everything old is new again. Collecting and reselling anything that is old — furniture, jewellery, books, newspapers, trading cards, clothes and so on — has become a major source of revenue for a large number of individuals.

Trading in nostalgia is ideally suited for home businesses. Not only is a fixed place of business unnecesary to sell the products, it is often restrictive. Shows, fairs, exhibitions and sales can be found at the nearest shopping centre, at downtown and suburban hotels and at flea markets everywhere. The stock in trade is hauled from home (or storage) to the show, set up and offered for sale, and unsold items return to home base to await the next sale. The management and administrative work is usually completed at home offices.

The fact that we live in a global village now means that regardless of where products are manufactured — locally, nationally, or internationally — they can usually be easily obtained for distribution from the home business. As with trading in nostalgia, opportunities to import or distribute products manufactured by others can be found in virtually any classified advertising section of any newspaper. Business opportunities can also be identified through leisure travel. Ideas and concepts that appear to be working effectively in distant locations can often be implemented at home.

Supplying Services

The service sector, if indeed such a separate sector exists, has experienced an extraordinary rate of growth over the past decade. In the past decade, 94% of all new jobs in the U.S.A. and Canada were created by the service industries — in retailing, business and financial services, engineering and design, consulting, commercial education and training, communication, travel and transportation.

By defining service to mean any act or labour that one person does for another that does not result in the ownership of anything tangible, it is clear that service is a component of all but the most basic of goods.

Services may be classified by identifying the end user.

Personal Services Provided To Individuals

These services are defined by the personal needs, wants and expectations of the person to whom the service is being provided. Generally speaking, the services are tasks that could be undertaken and completed by the recipient of the services if he or she had the time, talent and inclination.

Traditionally, personal services have included beauty and fashion related services such as hairstyling and make-up. With the growth of two income families, tasks traditionally performed by individuals for themselves have been "contracted out" to others. Many successful businesses now profitably provide services such as housekeeping, care-giving, home maintenance and gardening.

Today's busy people often find themselves with more money than time. As a result, new service opportunities proliferate at a staggering rate. Too busy to shop? You can hire a shopping service to do it for you. No time to plan a party or family event? A number of professional party planners would be more than pleased to assist. Typical Yellow Page directories list hundreds of personal services ranging from Acupuncturists through Make-up Artists to Yoga Instruction. New business opportunities continue to arise in response to our changing needs. One extreme example is the service provided by a Japanese business consulting and training company with the intriguing name of Japan Efficiency Headquarters. This company has developed a unique concept of providing personal services. It rents professional actors to visit elderly parents in the place of busy individuals and young couples. These actors serve as stand-ins for family visits, allowing the older family members to maintain some form of contact with their younger "family".

The home business environment is ideal for businesses that provide personal services. They all require a minimum of space and equipment and are based primarily on the personal skills and ability of the business operator. Once the requisite skills and tools of the trade have been acquired, the business operator can adopt the hired gunslinger's motto: "Have Tools, Can Travel". The services are delivered where the client needs and wants them. Management and routine administrative tasks are completed at the home office.

Services Provided To Business And Other Organizations

Businesses and not-for-profit associations purchase services for one of two reasons. The first is the simplest and most basic: to meet their own organizational needs and to operate and maintain the business as an organization. The second is to add information and/or knowledge to the business or organization.

Services of the first type would include obtaining and delivering inventory and supplies, running errands, taking messages, maintaining books and records and cleaning business premises. All business operations require these services to some extent; few require them on a full time basis. Since they require minimal equipment and space, these services can readily be provided by a home business. Although actual services, cleaning for example, are provided at the clients' place of business, the management and administration necessary to provide the services can be performed in a home office.

In many cases, the home business operator hires other people to do the actual work involved in providing the service. For example, other people obtain and deliver inventory and supplies, perform the bookkeeping tasks, etc. These people are paid less to perform the work than the client is charged for the service. Profit comes from the difference between the actual cost of providing the service and the fees charged to the customer.

In hiring other people to provide services, the role of the home business operator shifts. Instead of actually providing the services, he or she co-ordinates and supervises the delivery of services.

3 INFORMATION & KNOWLEDGE PRACTITIONERS

Capital is no longer the crucial asset in today's successful businesses. It has been replaced by information and knowledge. Competitiveness, formerly determined by the breadth and depth of the balance sheet assets of an individual business, is now determined in large part by the information available to a specific business and how this information is applied.

For purposes of the following discussion, it is helpful to distinguish between information and knowledge. To do this, information will be defined to mean:

"objective data or recorded details concerning some particular fact, subject or event".

Medical information would include text books and reported case histories; financial information would mean financial statements and other recorded and objective data.

Knowledge is defined as "**applied information**".

Thus, medical knowledge is applying or knowing how to apply medical information. A doctor gains her medical knowledge by applying information gathered from textbooks, case studies and clinical experience for the resolution of patients' difficulties. Financial advisors apply financial information to achieve desired results in specific situations.

Huge amounts of information on every topic known to humankind are generally available to anyone in the civilized world. You need not be an actuary to obtain actuarial tables. Similarly, you need not be a stock broker to obtain stock quotations. They are readily available to anyone who has access to the financial section of a newspaper. Technical manuals on the operation of everything from automobiles to synthesizers can be obtained in book stores and libraries.

The volume of information that a lay person can obtain is virtually limitless. However, the knowledge needed to apply information to real life situations is not part of the information itself. Actuarial tables are not self explanatory, nor are stock quotations or wiring diagrams for jet aircraft.

The knowledge needed to understand and apply information comes from study, training and hands-on experience. Just because I can read (and possibly understand) the stock market quotations, it doesn't follow that I can make prudent investment decisions. The knowledge required to do this comes from analyzing the information and synthesizing it with information from other sources. How many owners' manuals remain unread because the owner does not understand what he is reading much less know how to make practical use of the information?

Information is printed on paper, recorded on film or tape or recorded on microchips. Knowledge, on the other hand, can be considered to reside inside human brains individually and collectively. It develops from interest in work with information. This, in turn, results in experience which leads to increased knowledge.

Knowledge takes one of two forms. One form, which might be called pure knowledge, involves an understanding of what information means. The second form, applied knowledge, involves the practical application of information. For purposes of this discussion, the second form — applied knowledge — will be considered.

Opportunities for Home Business

All businesses deal with large volumes of information. Many employees are required to receive information and process it for use by others. Order clerks, for example, receive orders or purchasing information from customers and process it for use by production people. Other employees receive sales information and process it for use by finance or adminstration personnel.

Much of this information is processed using computers and telecommunications. Extensive downtown office premises and surrounding secretarial and support staff are seldom required. By connecting home computers with those located in downtown office complexes, or for that matter located hundreds of miles away, the tasks of processing information can be completed just as effectively from home offices as they can from centralized office complexes.

Employees of a business organization must use their individual and collective knowledge in applying information if the organization is to achieve its objectives. As noted, this knowledge resides inside the heads of skilled and experienced individuals. Thus, just as the task of processing information can be done from a home business, the task of applying it, can also be easily achieved from a home business.

The Information Explosion

New information is generated at such a rate that it is virtually impossible for any one person to keep abreast of everything that is happening in his or her field. We continue to be bombarded with information from a variety of sources: mass media, specialized and trade media, telecommunications including computer bulletin boards, facsimile machines, electronic mail and voice messaging. Little wonder that, individually and collectively, we show signs of information overload.

There are two common response strategies to the ongoing information explosion. First, we can screen out all information that is not directly and immediately relevant to us. Second, we can rely on others to do the screening and processing for us. In opting for the second strategy, we create the need for a specific group: information practitioners.

Information Practitioners

These are the people who work with information. Their work

ranges from initially gathering information to analyzing and synthesizing it and ultimately selecting and disseminating specific information to others. The following list outlines the various tasks of information practitioners.

Gathering Information

Essentially this task has two components: observing activities that can be seen or heard with relative ease and researching those activities that cannot be easily seen or heard. Observing activities means paying careful attention to what is happening and recording the observations in accordance with predetermined criteria.

Researching is a more focused approach. It involves one or more of these sub-tasks: investigating, identifying, surveying, classifying, interviewing, determining, identifying and reporting. Taking orders by telephone and market research are common business activities that are essentially information gathering tasks.

Comparing Information

Not surprisingly, with a large volume of information, there is much that is duplicated. Thus, it is often necessary to discover similarities and differences in batches of information.

Copying, Storing and Retrieving Information

There seems to be no end to the manual or automated methods of record keeping — posting, copying, transcribing, recording, protecting, filing, retrieving, reviewing and restoring of business information.

Computing Information

This task involves working with sets of numbers and data to produce new sets of numbers and data. Sub-tasks include: auditing, maintaining financial records, budgeting, projecting, calculating, purchasing, counting and reporting.

Advances in computer technology have simplified the completion of these sub-tasks.

Creating New Information

Creating new information is the process of transforming seemingly unrelated pieces and chunks of information into new cohesive relationships. Typical components of this process include integrating, unifying, innovating, hypothesizing, formulating, projecting and forecasting ideas and events. Preparation of a business plan as described in Chapter 14 shows how new information is created from apparently unrelated existing information.

Disseminating Information

Once created, information is distributed orally, in writing or electronically. Transmitting information orally is done through informed conversations and discussions or through formal speeches and presentations. Written or printed communications such as memos, letters, reports, books, magazines, newspapers and newsletters are common vehicles for distributing information in written format. Electronic communication includes television, radio and various telecommunication techniques such as computer bulletin boards and data bases, electronic mail and voice messaging.

Knowledge Practitioners

In and of itself, information is of little use to anyone. To be useful, information must be applied. It must be taken from the book or computer and employed in real life situations. This is the role of knowledge practitioners: to apply information that has been assembled by information practitioners. Frequently the information practitioner and the knowledge practitioner are one and the same person; the same person applies the information that he or she has gathered or created, acting in different capacities at different times.

The following list outlines the various tasks of knowledge practitioners.

Analyzing Information

A more advanced form of comparing information, analyzing information involves breaking a principle into its constituent parts or basic elements. Specific sub-tasks include evaluating, examining, extracting, selecting, testing and interpreting collected information. In essence, this task involves answering the question: what does all this information mean?

Communicating

The word "communicate" in all of its many forms is one of the most overused and misused words in our contemporary vocabulary. In the simplest of terms, communicating involves both sending and receiving a message. Communicating knowledge is dramatically different from simply disseminating information; it involves communicating the application of specific information. Its effectiveness depends largely upon the sender's awareness of what message is being sent and why, and an understanding of the receivers' needs, wants and expectations. Because communication involves sending and receiving a message, its effectiveness also depends upon the receiver, who must be ready, willing and able to receive the message sent. The vehicles of communication are the same as those used to disseminate information, i.e. orally, in writing, or electronically.

Advising or Consulting

Largely because of the information explosion, there is no end to the number of individuals and groups who are willing to advise and consult. Advising consists of providing specialized knowledge based on a broad range of available information. Consulting usually has the added elements of gathering, comparing, computing, analyzing, exchanging and creating new information over a period of time.

Training or Educating

This process is intended to provide new knowledge to others through lecture, demonstration or practice. It involves explaining complex batches of information, giving examples and demonstrating how specific information may be applied. Generally, it means helping others to develop new knowledge and skills.

Planning

All available information and knowledge is applied to the task of setting appropriate goals and identifying strategies that will achieve these goals. Aspects of the process include reviewing historical information of what has happened in the past and projecting what impact these results will have on future activities.

Implementing

Implementing a plan or executing a decision means putting it into action by applying the knowledge and instructions. The results are monitored to ensure achievement of the ultimate goals.

Information and Knowledge Practitioners — Working From Home

Following are illustrations of how these services can be provided from home offices.

Gathering Information

Unless the activities being observed are taking place in a controlled in-house setting, such as market research focus groups, observation usually takes place away from a central office. Reporting the observations can be done from the observer's home office with the actual report transmitted to a central facility by telephone modem, fax machine, courier or ordinary mail.

Surveying and interviewing can be done in person or by telephone. The home office can easily serve as a base from which the surveys and interviews are planned, implemented and co-ordinated. Research findings can be analyzed in the home office with the report transmitted as outlined above.

Processing Information

The tasks of processing and communicating or disseminating information can all be done from a properly computerized home office. Video recording equipment will be necessary to distribute video-based information.

Copying, Storing and Retrieving Information

Manual or automated record keeping, transcribing, recording and reviewing business information can easily be done from a home office. High rental rates for office and commercial space have led to the practice of storing closed files of hard copy material off-site in storage warehouses. If a specific file is needed, the warehouse operator is notified and one or more boxes of files is taken from the warehouse and forwarded to the office.

Whenever I have seen boxes of closed files stacked and awaiting either in-house searching or return to the warehouse, I have questioned the efficiency of the system. Surely a more efficient approach would be to dispatch a properly qualified and briefed individual to the warehouse to retrieve specific documents or information. Why couldn't qualified independent file clerks, working from home offices, retrieve and deliver individual files?

Advising or Consulting

As many practitioners are finding, these tasks are ideally suited for home businesses. Information is gathered and processed as outlined above. Advice and recommendations are prepared in the home office and communicated to the client.

Training

When necessary, training facilities can be rented from

hotels and from private and public educational institutions. Pre-training preparation and post-training follow-up can be completed from home offices.

In providing the above information and knowledge-based services as an independent contractor, the practitioner can enjoy all of the advantages of running a home business. There is also the added advantage of choosing one's client or clients.

Opportunities for Traditional Business Operations

Traditional business and related organizations can also reduce costs significantly by contracting services out to home based knowledge practitioners. The cost of the services will be limited to the services purchased since they do not include such overhead features as office space, computer equipment, secretarial and clerical services and employee benefits. As a result, home businesses can also be beneficial for traditional organizations.

4 WHAT'S RIGHT ABOUT HOME BUSINESS

A s noted above, there are many reasons why an individual would choose to start a home business. For the most part, these reasons are personal. They flow from the individual's lifestyle decisions and the circumstances surrounding his or her job or workplace.

From a purely business perspective, there are a number of factors that make home businesses attractive operational formats. These factors often combine to demonstrate what is right about home businesses.

The Efficiency Edge

Service that is primarily delivered by a single individual is more profitable and of higher quality if delivered from a home office. Here's why.

Today's large business organizations are products of the Industrial Revolution. Just as the economies of scale encouraged the development of larger and more automated factories, the perception that bigger is better encouraged the development of bigger business organizations. Larger factories and bigger business organizations required correspondingly large volumes of capital. Many businesses were seduced into believing that if they had enough resources — human, physical and financial — there would be virtually no limit to the volume of goods and services that they could sell. That balloon has burst.

The focus of our economy has shifted from the production of goods to the delivery of services. Today, the provision of service accounts for approximately 67% of domestic Gross

National Product.

Large factories and big business organizations now find themselves with extensive and expensive excess capacity. While "onward ever upward" was the doctrine of the past, downsizing is today's credo. Survival of the organization through cost reduction often takes precedence over client service. The situation has been exacerbated by the technological revolution working in conjunction with the dawning of the information age.

Today's information and knowledge practitioners do not need the costly resources of large organizations to serve their clients. Although attractive, chrome and marble office towers add little to actual client service. Nor do support staff such as coffee servers and mail clerks, efficient and helpful though they may be.

The argument that the resources of a large organization are necessary to serve clients is no longer valid. To provide service to clients, many people need only their own knowledge and access to a computer. A broad range of reasonably priced computer equipment and software is readily available. More specialized services and facilities such as telephone answering, book-keeping and meeting rooms are available on fee for service basis. In addition, a broad range of client services can be referred or subcontracted out.

In providing services from the home office, only those services that the client actually needs are delivered. Fees are based on the value of the service, not the revenue necessary to meet high overhead. Further, better quality service can be delivered because of the freedom from organizational considerations, internal competition and conflicting career plans.

The Manoeuvrable Edge

Large organizations are like the luxury liner *Queen Elizabeth II*; home businesses are like windsurfers. Establishing a home business requires little capital. Like the wind surfer, it requires neither an experienced crew nor sophisticated technology. It relies primarily on the knowledge and skills of the individual.

Operators of home businesses can maintain direct relationships with clients, eliminating virtually all of the dualisms listed in Chapter 8.

The simplicity of the home business makes it more man-oeuvrable than its big business competitors. In response to changing opportunities and conditions, a home business can take prompt and decisive action. Changes in direction can usually be done without additional resources or extensive consultation. In contrast, the sheer momentum of large organizations requires a major redeployment of resources and endless consultations to effect even the smallest observable changes. For example, it took the North American automobile industry several years to respond to their customers' demand for smaller cars. The mind boggles at the resources, both human and financial, required to respond to the shifting market demands.

The Intuitive Edge

The Oxford English Dictionary defines intuition as "...the immediate apprehension ...without the intervention of a reasoning process". It is the "aha" or "Eureka" of a sudden insight, often experienced at the most unexpected times.

Business is rich with examples of intuition-driven success stories. Ray Kroc, well known developer of the McDonalds Restaurant empire, is featured in one such story. In 1960 he offered to purchase the business and franchise rights from Richard and Maurice McDonald, the restaurant's original founders. The brothers quoted a price of $2.7 million and removed the original restaurant from the deal. Kroc's lawyer advised him not to pay the exorbitant price. Kroc listened to his own intuition: he called his lawyer back and said "take it". The rest, as they say, is history.

Former presidential candidate H. Ross Perot, a great believer in intuition, describes the term as "knowing your business...It means being able to bring to bear on a situation everything that you've ever seen, felt, tasted and experienced in an industry".

Whether it's playing a hunch or relying on good or bad feelings in making decisions, intuition is a significant and generally positive feature of our business environment.

The bad news about intuition is that it is not always a welcome feature. As discussed, today's big business organizations are legacies of the Industrial Revolution; they have developed the unshakable belief that bigger is better. They have also been greatly influenced by the scientific method, which encourages, logical, rational and provable thinking and decision-making. Deviations from these standards of bigness and linear thinking are unwelcome and unacceptable in business organizations. Although intuitive individuals may work for the biggies, they must often deny their intuition to ensure career advancement.

Such organizations have been called "The Enemy of Intuition":

> "Big organizations, and that includes governments, unions, and corporate oligopolies that submerge the individual, are clearly intuition's enemy. No boss can keep contact with everything that is going on, much less see down into the engine room of the organization where a head of antimanagement steam may be building. Communication from below is expressed impersonally in numbers plans and analyses and executive decisions are based on these abstractions....on lower levels, intuitive ideas are automatically tuned out. Eurekas are simply not a factor, because no credence is given to anything that can't be weighed, measured, and analyzed by computer..." [1]

The good news is that the simpler, less convoluted structure of home businesses is the ideal environment for intuition. Being able to bring to bear everything that he or she has ever seen, felt, and experienced in working with clients, enables the business person to draw fully on personal intuitive forces. Intuitive ideas need not be weighed, measured or analyzed by computer; they need only to serve the client better.

The Competitive Edge

Home businesses are also well positioned to develop and maintain a competitive advantage over larger business operations.

A more efficient and less cumbersome structure can deliver services more responsively and at lower cost than can larger businesses. The home business windsurfer can manoeuvre effectively to take advantage of new opportunities and to avoid upcoming difficulties.

The features that make home businesses so attractive in today's climate will continue to benefit home businesses in the future. Unlike the Industrial Age, in which vast amounts of capital were required to develop or acquire production tools, the Information Age will provide major opportunities for ordinary people with modest resources.

5 WHY HOME BUSINESS WILL THRIVE

We are living in a very challenging age. The nature of our entire world is changing at an unprecedented rate. It is virtually impossible to keep up with the latest trends. How can anyone understand the present, let alone forecast the future?

Fortunately, assistance is available from many sources. Among them is Faith Popcorn, who in her best selling book, *The Popcorn Report*[2] reports on what we will buy, where we will work and what we will think in the 1990s. Her own business was started and operates on what she had learned from her family's small business. Her company's client list includes many of the world's leading business organizations.

In his best selling work, *The Knowledge Value Revolution*,[3] Taichi Sakaiya prophesies a new economic and social order. Sakaiya, born in Tokyo, was a civil servant before becoming a writer and commentator of great influence in Japan and increasingly around the world.

What do these writers have to say about the present and the future that has significance for home businesses? The Popcorn Report outlines ten trends, four of which have direct relevance.

Cocooning

The term was initially coined to mean "...the impulse to go inside when it just gets too tough and scary outside. To pull a shell of safety around yourself so that you're not at the mercy of a mean unpredictable world..."[4] The increasing number of home businesses is evidence of this trend. As the number of such businesses increase, so will their credibility in the eyes of clients and potential clients.

Egonomics

Using the word "ego" — the individual — as its base, this trend indicates that "...everybody wants a little more attention, a little recognition of the 'no one is quite like me' self..." [5]

No longer satisfied with driving the same model black car, customers demand a wide range of models in a wide range of colours. Ironically, providing such choices eliminates the benefits to be gained from standardized mass production. Is it merely a coincidence that automobile manufacturers are losing vast amounts of money while at the same time increasing the range of models available? The manoeuvrability of home businesses enables them to respond more effectively and efficiently to clients' demand for individual recognition.

Cashing Out

This is the trend to "...slow down your racing heart beat and revive your weary soul...It's cashing in the career chips you've been stacking up these years and going somewhere else to work at something you want to do, the way you want to do it." [6] The Industrial Age drew workers from their homes to factories and offices. The ending of the Industrial Age is now releasing workers back to their homes. This will increase the number and diversity of home businesses. Through selective networking and referrals, home businesses can provide a broad range of services to clients.

Vigilante Consumer

This trend is best described in Faith Popcorn's own words:

"It's an action adventure story that strikes terror in the hearts of corporations everywhere (or should). Our heroine, one timid and trusting Tillie Consumer, changes her name to Attila and strikes out at evil in supermarkets and the marketing world everywhere: attacking trickery, hype, and sham with all the weapons she has at hand:

her telephone, her typewriter, her increasingly powerful pocketbook...The consumer is fighting back..."[7]

Being closer to their clients, home businesses are less likely to alienate Atilla and find themselves subject to her wrath. Indeed, they may be the beneficiaries of this wrath. If big organizations are seen to be bad, smaller organizations might be seen as preferable alternatives.

From a different and broader perspective Sakaiya observes and records many trends. Most are global with little direct application to home business operations. Two trends are, however, significant and worthy of note.

Light/Thin/Short/Small

"The prevailing outlook changed as the 1980s began. 'Light/Thin/Short/Small' was the slogan that defined a new aesthetic that made light, compact products all the rage. Suddenly the era when 'big' and 'beautiful' were practically synonyms was at an end."[8]

As a result of reduced demand, excess capacity, increased competition and decreased profits, we have seen large organizations in every economic sector undertake massive downsizing. Home businesses are the ultimate downsized business operation. They are very much a part of this trend; they will continue to thrive as the trend continues.

Research Trends

"Current research and development...tends to revolve around finding new ways to save energy, to create more adaptable and multifunctional products and to disseminate information."[9]

Home businesses are consistent with each of these research objectives. Working at home instead of travelling to traditional office premises requires less energy for commuter travel. Home offices represent very adaptable and multifunctional uses of resources, resources integrally involved in the dissemination of information.

Not Recession — Restructuring

Many observers have commented that we are not experiencing a world wide recession; we are in fact experiencing a major restructuring. The surprising collapse of the Berlin Wall followed by the equally surprising collapse of the Soviet Union and the changes in South Africa attest to this unprecedented worldwide restructuring.

No country or business operation is exempt from this widespread desire for change. Large organizations, such as General Motors, formerly thought to be secure forever, scramble to find workable survival strategies. Despite continuing high profit levels, banks and financial institutions struggle to deal with increasing numbers of problem loans to formerly blue chip clients.

Large business organizations are frequently unable to provide their employees with the once cherished security for life. This continued uncertainty in the big scene will continue to encourage talented individuals to flee to the security of their own home offices.

Taken collectively, these trends do not auger well for the traditional ways of doing things. There is ample evidence to suggest that the approaches that have worked so well in the past are not working as well now and will probably not work as well in the future.

New ways of doing things must be found. One of the most exciting and viable new approaches to profitable business operation is the home business. Enjoying an annual growth rate of 12%,[10] home businesses will be a major force in the future.

6 WHAT'S WRONG WITH BIG ORGANIZATIONS

Obviously, all business organizations should exist to serve their customers or clients. As an outsider to large business organizations, I once naively believed that this was as true of them as it was of smaller businesses. In my innocence, I also believed that the individuals who managed and directed large and apparently successful business operations understood what their clients wanted and needed and how to meet these wants and needs. After all, if they didn't know for sure, they certainly had the financial and human resources to find out.

My illusions were totally shattered when I joined a major professional services firm: the third largest of its kind in the country. It was here that I gained my first glimpse of the top of a large organization. Although I could no doubt fill the remaining chapters with examples, one specific example will suffice to illustrate my point.

The National Director to whom I reported was a constant source of frustration. He was responsible for the development of a new service area, one in which he had no direct hands-on experience. This, ironically, posed no internal difficulty. He considered himself an expert in the field, based exclusively on his having spent 4 years "managing" an office in which there were several people who actually had experience in the specific service area. Further, the executive partner to whom he reported had no hands-on experience either.

Although I had more experience in our particular service area than he and the rest of his staff combined, he never listened to my comments or seriously considered my reports. After one particularly frustrating exchange with the National Director, I had occasion to speak to another member of the firm, from another office. After allowing me to vent my anger and frustration, this person commented: "The *QE2* wasn't designed for racing." He went on to explain that the firm, as an organization, was much like Cunard Lines' luxury liner *Queen Elizabeth II*. Like the *QE2*, the firm can't change direction quickly. Its size prevents quick responses to changing circumstances. Its operating philosophy, although not officially expressed in writing, is stay the course. Its momentum eliminates factors inconsistent with its direction.

In a nutshell, my colleague's comments explain why many large business organizations cannot respond effectively to their customers' shifting demands. They are severely restricted by their size and momentum; even if they wanted to, they can't respond quickly to changing situations. (It is interesting to note that during the preparation of this book, in the summer of 1992, the *QE2* ran aground off the east coast of the USA. How many large organizations have run aground since?)

The View From the Top

The view from the top often precludes the ability of larger organizations to meet customer needs and wants effectively. There are many reasons why this view is somewhat distorted.

Focus

The view from the top is focused on others at or near the top, rather than on those lower down the ladder who are in fact closer to their customers. Information "from the trenches" consists of reports filtered and sanitized according to the needs of the organization rather than those of the clients.

Perspective

Like the office towers in which large organizations locate their head offices, most organizations are vertical or hierarchical in nature. To reach the top, one must work his or her way up the ladder.

This has a long term effect of encouraging an upward looking perspective. Individuals look up for direction or for information; they look up to see what those ahead on the ladder are doing, or to ensure that their career path is on track.

Because customers are perceived to be outside the company, an upward perspective tends to preclude looking outward at the clients.

Distance

The hierarchical nature of large organizations encourages internal layers and levels. Hence the expression "climbing the corporate ladder". It also creates significant psychological distances between the people at the top and those at the bottom.

Notwithstanding today's excellent communication technology, the psychological distance between top and bottom and between top and customer discourages effective communication. Further, the distance encourages those at the top to hear and believe what they want to hear and believe.

Career Path

Individuals within large organizations almost invariably have upwardly directed career goals. They want to move to the top. Upward mobility is more likely to follow internal political successes than outstanding client service activities. Not surprisingly, as individuals move up the career ladder, they in turn recognize the political successes of those below them in granting promotions and career advancements.

In the final analysis more people have made it to the top of their organizations through personal political prowess than through the ability to look after clients. This approach encourages politically driven careers and discourages careers that are driven by meeting clients' needs.

Walls Not Bridges

It has often been said that it's lonely at the top. This is because people at the top tend to build walls and not bridges. They protect themselves from the outside world, including clients, by security personnel, receptionists, secretaries, assistants, underlings and various physical barriers made of marble, glass, chrome and decorative woods and tapestries. It should not be surprising then, that the walled-in view from the top excludes serious consideration of client.

As on all passenger liners, there is a tradition on the *QE2* that the captain invites passengers to dine at his table. This puts him closer to his passengers, i.e. his customers. This in turn provides him with another perspective on what is happening on the ship. The customer's perspective is one that can be gained only by leaving the top, i.e. the bridge of the ship and going to where the passengers are.

This raises the question: What steps do other large organizations take to bring top management closer to the customers?

The Route to The Top

Few individuals have had the luxury of committing themselves clearly and unequivocally to quality customer service on their climb to the top. It is probably easier to teach an old dog new tricks than for people at the top of traditional business organizations to develop a genuine customer orientation. Given the training and background of many of the individuals at the top of organizations, this distorted perspective should not be surprising.

Lawyers at the Top

A large number of organizations have lawyers in top management positions. It is a commonly held view that lawyers are intelligent and analytical individuals, who are good at making decisions.

Unfortunately this view is more mythical than real. It is

unlikely that lawyers are any more intelligent than other highly trained individuals. Their analytical skills lead to the often terminal condition of "analysis paralysis". This in turn leads to decisions made by default, through frustration or expediency. Further, lawyers receive virtually no management or business training in law school. They can and do take strong adversarial positions on any side of any issue. Contemporary legal education focuses more on helping individual lawyers to protect themselves from clients than on helping them to meet clients' needs.

In view of all of this, why do lawyers continue to be found at and near the top of large organizations? Lawyers make excellent politicians. They thrive and prosper within the political culture of virtually any organization. Clients' perspective, if indeed present, is lost in their climb to the top. Once at the top, a lawyer will invariably use his or her skills to stay there rather than to ensure that customers' needs are met more effectively.

Accountants at the Top

Like lawyers, accountants are often found at or near the top of many organizations. With well developed financial skills, accountants are seen to be excellent candidates for top management positions.

However, there are significant differences between controlling finances and managing large organizations. The skills that are necessary for preparing and interpreting financial statements are not the same skills that are needed to identify clients' needs or for that matter to oversee a large organization. Further, managing cash flow is not usually the appropriate training and experience for meeting customers' non-financial needs.

Why then do accountants become top management people? Perhaps it is because many people see running a business simply as a means of spending money to generate more money. If such were indeed the case, accountants would be ideally suited for their positions at the top of organizations. In the real world, however, business is all about serving clients. Accountancy training focuses on the technical aspects of "number crunching" and "bean counting". Such training is hardly adequate for top management positions, which require a much wider range of skills.

Sales People at the Top

Thanks to their excellent sales skills, many sales people have managed to work their way to the top of their organizations. These people honestly believe that consumers, if left alone, will not ordinarily buy enough of their organizations' products. They initiate and thrive on aggressive selling and promotion efforts.

The same skills that have helped them to sell record-breaking numbers of widgets have helped them sell themselves into senior positions within their organizations. Throughout their careers, making the sale has been more important than product attributes or customer needs. These people have difficulty shifting their focus from making the sale to identifying and meeting customer needs. Their organizations likewise reflect this difficulty.

Production People At The Top

A number of production people have also risen to the top of their organizations. These people believe that customers will favour those products that are widely available and low in cost. They concentrate on achieving high production efficiency and wide distribution coverage.

They may also believe that customers will favour those products that offer the most quality, performance and features. They focus their energy on making good products and improving them over time. The customers themselves, are however, important only in so far as they relate to the product; their actual needs and wants play little role in the decision making process.

Organization People At The Top

This is the modern day equivalent of the organization man: the person who started at the bottom, classically in the mail room, and through a lifetime of devotion to the company has managed to make it the top. They know all about the organization. Its history, culture and traditions are all part of the family lore. Through their years of dedication and devotion to the organization they have earned their position at the top. In return, these people provide the organization with their undying loyalty and gratitude.

They give priority to protecting the organization, its history and its traditions. Criticism of the organization is considered negative rather than an opportunity for improvement. In the final analysis, organizational priorities are more important than those of the customers.

Just as the captain of the *QE2* is too far removed from the point at which the rudder hits the water, top management of large organizations is too far removed from their own organizations' equivalent: where the organization meets the customer. The route to the top, like the view from the top distorts or even excludes the customers' perspective. Is it any wonder that brave proclamations about the importance of customer satisfaction aside, shoddy customer service persists?

7 WHERE DOES THE CLIENT FIT?

The environments of large organizations are ideal breeding grounds for the twin maladies of dualism and empire building. Each interferes with looking after clients.

Dualism

Dualism is the phenomenon that creates we-they polarities. The polarities reflect opposing extremes, often considered to have little potential for peaceful co-existence. There are many possible dualisms. The following list outlines examples from A to Z. If you have ever worked in a large organization, you will recognize at least 5 of them.

Dualisms From A to Z

Adminstration vs Client Service

The administrative function looks after the organization's needs; client service function looks after delivery of services to clients. Hardly a day goes by without some conflict between these two functions. As a rule, the organization's needs are given priority attention at the expense of client service.

Big vs Small

Supporters of big organizations boast a full range of in-house resources to provide a broad variety of services. Small organizations claim to provide fewer but more specialized services. In both cases the focus is internal

— on the organization's resources, rather than external — on the client's needs.

C lient vs The Organization

Clients are often seen as outside forces interfering with the otherwise smooth operation of a business. How often have you heard a client start a telephone conversation with "I'm sorry to bother you but..."? Worse yet is the expression "I know how busy you are so I referred my friend to someone else." In one form or another, the message of being too busy to look after clients comes directly from the organization.

D owntown vs Suburban

Although more costly, downtown locations are seen, at least by downtown people, as being more important or more prestigious. Conversely, suburban locations are perceived as being more cost efficient and more user friendly.

E ntrepreneur vs Bureaucrat

The entrepreneur is creative and more of a risk taker. Conversely, the bureaucrat clings to established systems and procedures and avoids risks. Where do clients' interests fit?

F ield vs Head Office

People in the field claim to be close to customers and know what they really want; they believe that head office personnel just don't understand clients. Conversely, head office personnel profess a broader view, preferring to consider clients as but one of many more global factors.

G eneralist vs Specialist

A generalist has a little knowledge and information about many things; a specialist has a great deal of knowledge and information about a few things. Both approaches are necessary for client service.

H ome vs Office

Thanks to modern technology, many office functions such as data or word processing, can be performed very satisfactorily from employees' homes. For reasons of control and habit, managers and supervisors still require that these functions be performed in the organization's office.

I nternal vs External

Individual components in the process of delivering services, such as printing and copying, can either be produced internally or contracted out and purchased from external sources. A variation on the "do we make it or buy it?" question, this dualism can affect every person within an organization. The decision should, but is not always, made on the basis of what is best for the client.

J oint vs Separate

Joint projects involving more than one individual, group or business organization can create a synergy that benefits all concerned. Working on projects separately ensures consistency in planning, implementation and control. Depending on the circumstances either approach can be the most advantageous for the client.

K ids vs Oldtimers

The classic youth versus age conflict, this dualism includes all aspects of youth opposing all aspects of age. Rather than being mutually exclusive, these extremes complement each other extraordinarily well. Oldtimers can pass their experience on to the kids; kids can share their energy and idealism with the oldtimers making possible new insights into old problems.

L ow Price vs High Quality

Supporters of low pricing policies believe customers' purchase decisions will be made primarily on the basis of price. Conversely, fans of quality believe that customers' decisions are driven by quality considerations. As is the case with most dualisms, both positions are right and both are wrong. The challenge is to profitably deliver quality at a price that the customer is willing to pay.

M arketing vs Sales

The goal of a marketing orientation is ensuring customer satisfaction in the long run; the goal of a sales orientation is simply increasing the volume of sales.

N orth vs South

Regional differences between north and south or between east and west are perhaps the biggest source of we-they divisions. This is true whether you are considering an organization, a country or our entire global village.

O ut of Town vs In Town

This often raises the question: "Do we buy out of town (province, country) for better price (quality, variety, etc) or shop locally to support our local suppliers?"

P rofessional vs Support Staff

Legal, accounting and consulting firms all foster this distinction. Most create additional divisions such as senior partner, junior partner, associate, manager. Other large organizations use similar distinctions such as management vs labour that foster divisiveness.

Quiet vs Background Music

Some people prefer quiet and peaceful environments; others require background music. The middle ground in this dualism seldom satisfies anyone.

Right vs Left

Although a political concept, the right versus left axis applies equally to most business organizations. The right represents a traditional, more conservative philosophy; the left represents a more liberal and change oriented approach.

Sales vs Service

Automobile dealers visually demonstrate the difference between sales and service; they provide separate entrances, if not facilities for each.

Technology vs Individuals

Initially associated with the Industrial Revolution, these areas of concern continue to be a major source of conflict in many business organizations. Undoubtedly, many individuals have been inconvenienced, even losing their jobs to new technology. Equally true, new technology has created new employment opportunities for many, including operators of home businesses.

Urban vs Rural

Personnel in urban centres like to think of themselves as more knowledgable and well informed than their "country bumpkin" counterparts in rural centres. Conversely, personnel in rural centres like to think that they are closer to their clients and can provide better service than their stressed out city counterparts.

Variable vs Standard

Today's clients demand that the services that they purchase meet their own specifications. Each client considers himself unique. Thus each service offering must be customized to meet the needs of each individual customer. The operating efficiency of big organizations depends upon the delivery of standard services. Thus, decisions about delivery of service must often balance profitability with meeting specific client needs.

Winners vs Losers

A feature of competition is that there are winners and losers. Losers in internal political struggles have difficulty in securing the resources necessary to properly serve their clients.

Xerox vs The Others

The Xerox company developed the photocopy process. Others have followed suit. Many Xerox customers have developed a long term loyalty. However, there may be times to consider other options. Conflicts between loyal Xerox supporters and "alternative seekers" often develop when this approach is suggested.

Yesterday vs Tomorrow

An organization must be aware of its past, its heroes, its ideals, it successes and its failures. It is, however, all too easy to get stuck there. Without a vision of the future, the organization and its members will stagnate.

Zealous vs Apathetic

A zealous approach to client service is eager and enthusiastic. It asks: "What can we do for you today?" The apathetic approach...doesn't really matter.

The existence of these dualisms is inevitable and should be no more of a problem for large organizations than conflicting demands are for individuals. If individuals adopt extreme or uncompromising positions, the different polarities create at least two major difficulties. First, dealing with the consequences of extreme and strongly held positions drains resources of time, energy and money from other, more productive activities.

Second, customers are often caught in the middle of these battles. Many customers will leave as a result; those who stay may become innocent victims.

Given the significant consequences of internal differences, why do large organizations allow the dualisms to continue?

Empire Building

Dualisms often lead to or flow from empire building. In the climb to the top of the ladder, increasing one's territory — empire building — is seen to be a positive achievement. As individual empires increase in size and influence, it becomes increasingly important to secure each empire from attempted takeover by other empire builders. Distinguishing one's own empire from others is seen to be a good defensive strategy. Creating we-they distinctions makes it easier to tell the good guys ("we") from the bad ("they"). Such distinctions make it less difficult to protect one's own empire, garner support from within, and strike alliances with other non-competing empires. Yet again the question is: where do the customers fit into all of this manoeuvring? The answer: they probably don't.

Protect Thy Backside (PTB)

Personal security has become a very important issue for most members of contemporary society. Security is a concern for every aspect of business operations, from parking lots to computers, from people to premises.

It is this obsession with security that gives rise to the PTB syndrome. Security in this case refers to job security within a large organization.

The physical symptoms of this syndrome include severe paper overburden and compulsive attention to recording each detail of every action. Behavioral manifestations include indecisiveness, buck passing, and confusing, often ambiguous speech patterns.

The syndrome arises out of real or perceived external or internal threats to an individual's well being. External threats might come from government and other regulatory agencies, competing business organizations, public interest or consumer groups, or customers.

Internal threats include superiors, subordinates and colleagues. Because any of these individuals might interfere with one's progress to the top, they must not be upset over anything.

Regardless of whether the threats come from outside or inside the organization, the end results are the same. In fact, the results are similar to the results of dualism, discussed above. Considerable resources are committed to wordy self-serving reports and evasive self-protection activities. Once again, customers are forgotten while individuals within an organization focus on protecting themselves and their positions.

In the simplest terms, large organizations are not well suited to properly serve their clients. The view from the top is distorted and the career path to the top is too internally focused to facilitate the development of an external or client orientation. Structurally, large organizations present ideal breeding environments for dualism and empire-building, each of which seriously interferes with looking after clients.

Can big organizations correct these problems? Many have tried; some have succeeded. Most, like the dinosaur and his relatives, simply can't make the necessary changes.

8 QUALITY SERVICE — A CRITICAL BUSINESS STRATEGY

At Ford, Quality Is Job 1 and It's Working.
At Zenith, The Quality Goes In Before The Name Goes On.
At McDonalds, Quality is Guaranteed.

Why All This "Quality" Talk?

"Quality is the most important strategic issue facing top management in the 1990s. What we mean by quality is more than the traditional notion of quality in products and services...It is a bottom line issue that addresses the very roots of a business, and it requires a change in thinking from the top of an organization to the bottom. To put it succinctly, there is a strong correlation between quality and profitability." [11]

This quotation demonstrates the importance of quality in today's marketplace. Many contemporary business organizations see quality improvement as their salvation.

Modern principles of quality management were first introduced in Japan following World War II. As a result, the Japanese economy has grown from post-war devastation to global pre-eminence. Many North American companies have followed the Japanese lead in trying to manage quality. Some organizations have found it to be a very effective operating philosophy.

For most large organizations, all of this quality talk remains just that: talk. Despite the bravest of intentions, and the expenditure of millions of dollars, the general culture and individual environments of large organizations remain anti-quality. The management structure of most business organizations is such that their employees couldn't deliver quality client service — even if they wanted to. In trying to provide quality service to clients, employees are often caught between supervisors whose personal agendas focus on self preservation, and inadequately trained support staff who may not know the meaning of quality.

For the home business, the significant element of the above quotation is the sentence, "... To put it succinctly, there is a strong correlation between quality and profitability." Free of non-supportive supervisors and support staff, home businesses can ensure quality client service to all clients, all of the time. In fact, the quality of client service can actually be better than that of larger competitors.

A Brief History of The Quality Movement

Quality Improvement In Prehistoric Times

Interest in quality improvement is not new. In fact, our earliest ancestors devoted a great deal of energy and ingenuity to improving the quality of their lives. Seeking shelter in caves and learning to use fire are two examples. Similarly, the introduction of irrigation to farming was directed at improving the quality of the land in order to produce more and better crops.

As families began living together in communities, their changing life-styles were matched by changes in what they did and how they did it. They learned that goods of better quality had a higher trading value than goods of standard quality. Craftsmen and tradesmen who produced similar goods joined together to develop guilds or associations for the purpose of establishing and maintaining quality standards for the goods that they produced. The seal or mark of the guild was seen to be a guarantee of quality; goods bearing the guild seal were considered to be of higher quality than those goods produced by non-members of the guild.

Quality In The Industrial Revolution

Although the Industrial Revolution created a shift in

emphasis from quality to quantity, quality was not totally forgotten. Through the increased use of more sophisticated machinery, manufacturers were able to reduce the per unit costs of producing an increased volume of goods. Although perhaps not the same standard of quality of goods as hand-produced by craftsmen, mass produced goods were considered to be of "acceptable quality" to the customer.

Reduced in importance, quality continued to be an important force into the twentieth century.

Quality In The Twentieth Century

As with so many other important developments, twentieth century quality management can trace its beginnings to agriculture. To improve crop growing methods, Britain's R.A. Fisher analyzed bushels of data to identify cause-and-effect relationships between planting activities and harvest yields. Fisher's work was the foundation for that of Walter A. Shewhart, a physicist at AT&T Bell Laboratories. Shewhart is credited with transforming Fisher's work into a quality control discipline for factories. Shewhart's work in turn inspired W. Edwards Deming and J.M. Juran, today's pre-eminent champions of quality.

Despite their differences, both Deming and Juran made a significant contribution to Japan's remarkable post war recovery. While American manufacturers were pulling out all the stops to meet the post war demand for consumer goods, the Japanese were focusing on the importance of quality. This concern, some would say obsession, has enabled Japan to develop into an economic powerhouse, outperforming the American economy on many fronts. As a result of this extraordinary success, this geographically small country with virtually no natural resources has become the centre of attention in a world once again interested in the benefits of quality.

Quality in the 1990s

The "flavour-of-the-month" world of current business theory has spawned innumerable experts on the subject of quality. Since 1990, more than 200 books have been written on the subject, with one publisher alone listing 10 quality related titles in its fall 1992 catalogue. Every major business and trade publication has devoted considerable space to the importance of and role of quality. A whole new jargon has developed; phrases like Acceptable Quality Level (AQL), Continuous-Improvement Process (CIP), Quality Function Deployment (QFD) abound.

In short, quality has become the snake oil of the decade, the cure-all for all manner of management problems: low revenues, high costs, fierce competition, low staff morale etc. The rationale behind this cure-all approach seems to be that if quality management worked so well in post-war Japan in view of that country's overwhelming problems and lack of resources, it should work even better for us with fewer (or at least different) problems and more resources.

Today, all business organizations profess a commitment to quality. Many have implemented a formal program of quality management of some kind. Some of these organizations have actually succeeded in their endeavour. Those that have succeeded tend to be smaller and flatter in organizational structure with an overall operating philosophy that encourages employee participation and team work.

Unfortunately, the operating structure and environment of most big businesses remain anti-quality. Key decision makers are attracted by all of the attractive benefits of adopting quality programs, but their acceptance is usually subject to the number one priority of protecting and enhancing their own self interests.

On a more positive note, today's widespread interest in quality yields significant benefits to smaller businesses in general and home businesses in particular. It can, in fact, give a significant competitive advantage to home businesses.

Supplying Quality Service from Home Businesses

As we shift from the product oriented marketplace of the Industrial Age to the service oriented market of the Information Age, the importance of the service component attached to products becomes increasingly important. Products are sold on the basis of services promised and delivered. The duration of the power train warranty on a new automobile is as much a selling point as is the performance of the power train itself.

The service component of products sold by home businesses is equally important. It is the service component that often distinguishes products provided by home businesses from those provided by larger businesses. Personal service at home from a knowledgeable Avon, Fuller Brush or Tupperware representative is usually vastly superior to the uninformed indifference often displayed by clerks in larger shopping centres and department stores.

Regardless of the product provided by the home business, it is the quality of the service accompanying the product that is important. For the most part, the home business environment is free of the factors that make quality service so difficult for large. The common sense principles of quality client service are free to operate.

The following three chapters address these common sense principles. The basic concepts are as simple and inexpensive to implement in home businesses as they are complex and costly to realize in large organizations. They are the tools with which a home business can beat the biggies.

9 TEN BASIC TRUTHS ABOUT CLIENT SERVICE

Although there may be some similarities, providing clients with service is dramatically different from providing them with goods. The following truths outline the main differences.

1 Clients don't want the service itself; they want the benefits of the service.

This is particularly true of most professional services. Except for the occasional person who thrives on the attention that comes from medical treatment or court actions, most clients don't want these services any more than they would voluntarily purchase the services of dentist or an auto body shop.

What clients really want is the benefits that come from the service. These benefits may include help in resolving a problem or assistance in acquiring information, or even purchasing knowledge or skills that they lack. Benefits that might reasonably be expected as a result of purchasing dental services would be healthier, more attractive teeth. Similarly, the benefits arising from auto body shop services would include the repair and use of a damaged motor vehicle.

2 Clients need your service.

Clients will usually consider their internal resources before going outside to purchase services. This means that you are not your clients' first choice. They need you to perform some task that they are unwilling or unable to perform for themselves.

Thus, the services that you ultimately deliver to clients are defined by your clients' needs. Services could be the performance of specific tasks such as writing an operations manual or preparing advertising copy. Alternatively, the services could involve providing specialized information and knowledge such as a summary of attractive investments. In many cases, the services involve both providing information and performing specific tasks, such as summarizing potential investments and then purchasing investments on the client's behalf.

3 Clients demand quality service.

As noted in the previous chapter, the demand for quality service is widespread in our contemporary society. This demand is just as commonplace with business people as it is with consumers.

It results from two forces working simultaneously. Business people are also consumers. As such, they are like everyone else bombarded with advertising that emphasizes quality as a vital component of fast food, cars, home appliances, housing, travel accommodations and so forth. The message is bound to spill over into their work. If quality is an important component of their personal lives, should it not also be a component of their work lives? If the products they purchase as consumers are "quality checked" should they settle for anything less at work?

The second force is the increasing number of business organizations currently adopting formal quality programs. Total Quality Management or TQM, is becoming one of the most popular buzz-words of the nineties as organizations large and small adopt quality driven philosophies. A key TQM principle requires suppliers, e.g. you and your competitors, to provide evidence of their ability to deliver quality goods and services. Failure to provide this evidence will put you at a serious disadvantage in competing with those who can provide it.

4 Quality service is what your clients say it is.

Many retail businesses have posted signs with the following rules of customer service:

Rule #1: The customer is always right.
Rule #2: If you think the customer is wrong, read Rule #1.

This is one way of defining quality service. If your standards of quality coincide with or exceed your clients' standards, you will be successful. If your standards fail to meet those of your clients, you risk losing their business.

A cautionary note: clients' standards may be unrealistic for different reasons. They may not fully understand what they require from you. They may also not fully understand what you can and cannot do for them. It is your responsibility to ensure that the client understands your services and the standards of quality that may be reasonably expected.

5 Providing technical information is not quality service.

Generally speaking, most clients are looking for more than technical information.

Whenever I consider purchasing new software for my computer system, I am not really looking for a lecture on the technical specifications of the latest version of a specific piece of software. There is no point in telling me about such seemingly exciting features as the improved speed of Windows 3.1 over Windows 3.0 or why a 486 whatever is better than a 386 with 33MHZ. I couldn't care less about these features because I simply don't understand what they mean. What I do care about is whether a particular piece of software will perform specific functions for me on my particular system.

Quality service in this situation consists of listening to what I am asking, and applying whatever technical information may be relevant to answering my questions in terms that I can understand. Like most consumers, I am usually ready to purchase when I understand what I am buying and what benefit I will receive.

The same principles apply regardless of the field. Do not simply recite technical information to clients: draw on your knowledge to help them understand how the technical information can be applied in their unique situations. Ensure that your clients fully understand the benefits that can reasonably be expected as a result of your service.

6 Clients do not always understand your technical jargon.

As we become more familiar with technical information we learn to communicate with our colleagues and peers in a form of oral shorthand or jargon. Consultants perform "SWOT analyses", financial analysts "crunch some numbers", psychologists administer a "WISC-III" and so on. To those in the know, the meaning of these terms is perfectly clear. To the uninitiated, they are gobbledygook. Communicating with clients involves treading a fine line between using terminology that is too technical on the one hand, and talking down to the client by using language that is too simple on the other. This underlines the importance of knowing and listening carefully to each individual client.

Knowing the client will enable you to assess what the client knows now and what he needs to learn in order to make a decision. It will also enable you to frame your questions and comments in terms and words that your client will understand.

7 Standardized technical services will produce comparable results, regardless of the provider of the service.

This is true of every standardized service area. Different insurance brokers will provide policies with analogous features. Although independent, they act as sales agents for the same insurance companies. Similarly, assuming they follow the same procedures for the same purposes, independent researchers will produce similar results. They are after all, considering the same information base.

Fortunately, the further one moves away from standardized services, the easier it becomes to distinguish services from those of the competition. The services of individual consultants are defined by their unique skills, knowledge and experience. Thus, two individual consultants may offer quite different but equally workable solutions for the same problem. The best solution is clearly the one that works best for the client.

8 Client service is intangible

As noted, services are intangible: they cannot be seen, tasted, felt, heard or smelled before they are purchased. This means that clients who are considering the purchase of services must draw inferences of quality indirectly.

In the case of large organizations, this means looking at physical premises, personnel, equipment, communications material, symbols and logos, and the price of the service. In home businesses, the range is limited to you, your communications material, your symbols and logos and your pricing. Presumably, clients can use these features to evaluate or predict the quality of the service.

9 Client service is variable

Because service cannot be mass produced on an assembly line, the same service can vary from one provider to another. Although it is true that all hair stylists receive the same basic training, they would be unlikely to create the same hair style for a specific client.

In less standard service areas such as consulting, there is considerable variance from consultant to consultant. With no uniform training and continuing education standards, consultants are free to provide whatever services that they believe will sell. In situations like this, any standardization or consistency of service standards is usually more by coincidence than design.

Service provided by any individual may also vary from time to time. As human beings, we are vulnerable to a broad range of physical, social and emotional factors that can affect our performance. A generally positive mood is more likely to result in better service than a negative mood.

10 Client service is perishable

Services cannot be produced and stored in inventory until they are needed. They are produced and used virtually simultaneously. This often results in service providers experiencing significant peaks and valleys during the year. For example, businesses that prepare tax returns face high demand for their services between February and April and low demand between July and September.

10 WHAT ARE CLIENTS REALLY LOOKING FOR?

Simple answers to complex questions are found in the most unexpected places at the most unexpected times. As I began consideration of the question "what are clients really looking for?" I felt totally intimidated by the mountains of market research that have accumulated on the topic. As the task of analyzing and digesting this mass of material appeared more and more onerous, I did what most reasonable people would do: I abandoned the chore and went on to do something else. It was while I was doing other things that I had a flash of insight from a seemingly different and unrelated source.

The insight came from a long-ago situation in which I was working with a client who was struggling to keep his small bakery business operating. As my client outlined his many-sided predicament, I was became overwhelmed by the task of finding solutions to his problems. There was hardly an area in which he wasn't facing serious problems: his bank and suppliers were pushing him for money; his customers were demanding more varied and better quality products; he thought that one of his employees was stealing from him; and as if to confuse the situation even further, his wife was threatening to leave him if things didn't improve. Although he came to me for advice, I did not know which of the many problems had the highest priority, let alone what advice to give.

In desperation, after allowing my client talk for what seemed an inordinately long time, I took a step that was most unusual for professionals in general, and for advisors in particular. I simply asked him what he wanted. After recovering from the shock, he was able to articulate an answer: he wanted to bake bread.

In hindsight I realized that my part in the discussion was to help my client identify what he was looking for and to help him understand what I could and could not do for him. As a result, we developed the ideal service situation: I knew what he wanted and he knew what I could do. From that point, I was able to get on with the task of helping him to arrange his affairs so that he could do what he wanted to do: bake bread.

In performing this task, it was necessary to direct my client's thinking through properly formulated and focused questions. Open ended questions, not answerable with a simple yes or no, allowed my client to discuss his situation with few constraints. Closed questions, requiring a simple yes or no answer, allowed me to focus on specific issues. As a result, it was possible to gather all of the information about the client and his situation that was necessary to develop and implement a proper course of action. (When I last spoke to this client, he was happily working as a baker in a small resort hotel, owned and operated by friends of his new spouse.)

Knowledge

My client came me with a problem to be solved. The knowledge that I provided through hearing him out and helping to clarify what he wanted, was a clearer understanding of the problem and of what I could or could not do about it.

This approach has worked remarkably well in other service situations. Your clients are coming to you because they have a problem or issue with which they need help. They are looking for two types of knowledge. First, they need to know what you can, and cannot, do to help them. Be honest with yourself and your client. If you can help, tell them what you can do. Conversely, if you cannot help them, tell them you so and offer to help them find some one else who can help them.

Second, they need your knowledge, or ability to create new knowledge, about their unique situation. This is what you will ultimately be selling to them. If the client had the knowledge or ability, it is unlikely that he or she would be coming to you in the first place.

Reliability

This is the ability to provide what you promised to your client, dependably and accurately. This could be as simple as calling the client at a specific hour on a specific day or as complex as a review of a situation within a set period of time.

We live in a cynical age. Ordinary people have been fooled or lied to far too often. We are tired of public figures promising one thing and doing something else. Clients don't expect the moon — they are not stupid; they know that you can not and will not deliver. They do, however, expect you to deliver, dependably and accurately, what you have promised.

Responsiveness

Clients expect you to be willing to help them and to provide timely service. If your service is not prompt, you will not remain in business for long.

Assurance

Assurance is the result of your knowledge and courtesy combined with your own ability to convey trustworthiness and confidence. It has often been said that there are two ways to appear knowledgeable. One is to read and understand all the literature that is available. The other is to be quiet and let the other person believe that you are knowledgeable. At the early stages of dealing with clients, the latter is the preferred approach. Just as I learned to allow my clients to have their say, many other professionals have learned to allow their clients to talk about their own problems. As well as appearing knowledgeable and interested, you can gain valuable insights from hearing clients talk about their problems in a seemingly undirected manner. Very often your own objectivity enables you to develop a solution to the client's problem as you listen.

In framing questions, use words and terms that you know your clients will understand. Your approach should be conversational rather than adversarial. The purpose of asking the questions is to obtain information from the clients, not to prove that you are right and the client is wrong. There is little to be gained by winning the argument but losing the client.

Empathy

Empathy is reflected in the degree of caring and individual attention you provide to clients. Although one of the important of client expectations to meet, this is often the most neglected.

The simplest method of demonstrating that you care about your clients is to listen to them. Instead of trying to impress clients with jargon and self-serving monologues, try listening to them. Allow them to tell you their story; let them tell you what it is they want. As you listen, don't engage in mental arguments with them or look for further opportunities to demonstrate your own skills and knowledge. Listen to try to understand what they are telling you. Ask questions to help you and your clients better understand what they need from you.

Operating your business from your home can provide you with a significant advantage in providing individual attention to clients. Because you will usually meet your clients away from your own place of business, you will be free of distracting files, telephone calls and other interruptions that are common in traditional businesses settings. Thus you should be able to devote all of your attention to the client.

Tangibles

This refers to your appearance and that of everything that you use and produce in dealing with clients. Once again, you have a distinct advantage over larger businesses. You determine how you should dress to meet with clients. You also have total control over the appearance of your tools and work outputs. You prepare all written material — proposals, reports, correspondence or whatever — the way you think best. You, not someone else in a large organization, have the full responsibility for presenting yourself and your work as competent, professional and sensitive to client needs.

What Clients Are Not Looking For

- Lectures on how their problems could have been prevented. 20/20 hindsight is of little use to anyone.
- Monologues and war stories that serve only to feed your ego and demonstrate how smart you think you are.
- Unrealistic promises that cannot possibly kept.
- Excuses for promises that were not kept.
- Indifferent and slow responses to their requests.
- Your concerns about your own insecurities or lack of knowledge.
- Interrogations and arguments.
- Second class treatment.

II WHAT YOU CAN DO FOR YOUR CLIENT

The previous three chapters addressed quality in general and how it relates to clients and their expectations. The following material outlines how you can meet these expectations.

Deliver Quality Service

The following five steps will help you to ensure that you consistently deliver quality service to your clients.

Step One: Listen To Your Clients

Your clients know their respective businesses better than you do. They also know their problems better than you do. What they may not know is how to describe their problems to you. They may not know what you can do to help them.

By listening carefully to what your clients say, you can learn a great deal. Through careful questioning you can help them describe their problems so that you can help develop a solution. You can also learn what your clients need to know about you.

Step Two: Identify and Meet Your Clients' Needs

Remember that your clients come to you because they require your assistance in meeting a specific need. Don't assume that just because you have identified a need, it is the one for which the client seeks assistance. In discussing the main issue, the client might be disguising the real issue — the one with which he really wants your help. The needs that you have identified and perceive as being important may not be the same needs that your client perceives as being important.

Once the needs are identified, and you and your client have agreed that these are the ones to be addressed, it is time to discuss a plan of action. This should include what you will and will not do, what the client will do, how long you expect the process to take, and how much you expect it will cost. It is prudent to over-estimate time and expense; this allows for flexibility in case of unexpected complications and lessens the likelihood of unpleasant or embarrassing surprises.

Step Three: Exceed Clients' Expectations

Your client will now have a set of expectations regarding the delivery of your service. Just as you commit yourself to meeting your client's needs, you should make a commitment to yourself to exceed his expectations. This means providing the service better, faster or less expensively than the client expected.

Step Four: Eliminate Variables

This step presents a significant challenge. On the one hand, the client expects and deserves unique non-standard service.

On the other hand, standardizing non-client service factors makes for greater efficiency and profitability. These factors include formats for reports and correspondence, procedures for gathering and analyzing information and practices involving billing and collecting accounts. It is not necessary, nor is it profitable, to continuously re-invent the wheel.

Step Five: Continuously Improve Your Service

As a service provider, you are only as good as the last service that you provided. Regardless of how good it was, undoubtedly there were areas where it could have been improved. Using the material in Chapter 17, ask for your clients' opinions as to how your service can be improved.

Other businesses, from automobile manufacturers to restaurant operators, use client input for improving their service. You should follow their lead.

Provide Appropriate Knowledge and Skills

The technological revolution and information explosion which have combined to open the door to home offices have also given rise to "instant experts". With access to an astounding volume of information, these individuals profess expertise in a broad range of areas. They often fail to realize that clients have access to the same information. What the clients need is the knowledge or skills that renders specific information applicable to their unique situations.

The client doesn't need you repeating information to her; she needs your knowledge of how current legislation or government regulations apply to her unique situation. She already knows about the importance of customer satisfaction; she needs your skills to help train her employees in new approaches to customer service.

Deliver What You Promise; Don't Promise What You Can't Deliver

As consumers, we are exposed to more than 3,000 commercial messages daily. Most of these messages promise worthwhile benefits if we will purchase a particular product or service. The range of promises covers all conceivable needs and wants.

Unfortunately, most of the promises are undeliverable. Regardless of its ultimate brightness and whiteness, a clean laundry is unlikely to result in a happier family. Drinking the right beer is not likely to dramatically improve one's social life or overall enjoyment of life. And so it goes: buy this product and your life will be measurably better.

Because consumers know better, they seldom believe un-believable promises offered by advertisers. They have been fooled before and do not wish to be fooled again.

The same considerations apply to politicians and other public figures. As members of the public, we have been deceived too often by too many people. We believe few, if any public promises.

Clients, like the consumers they are, are cynical when it comes to promises. They are unlikely to believe you when you promise anything. Promise whatever you choose — the proof is in the delivery. The same strategy that applies to client expectations (ensure they are reasonable and then exceed them) applies to promises. Ensure that your promises are realistic and then deliver more (better or faster) than promised. After you have developed a proper track record for delivering as promised, your clients will consistently believe your promises.

Of course, the corollary to this rule is not to promise what you can't deliver. Just because your client expects a piece of work to be done by tomorrow at 9:00 am, doesn't mean that you can do it. Ensure that your promises match your abilities and resources.

Ensure Timeliness Of Service

Our modern conveniences have moved from the labour saving stage to the instant age. Instant-on television sets eliminate the few seconds of warm-up time required by conventional sets. Thanks to microwave ovens, we can enjoy gourmet macaroni and cheese in 4 minutes rather than the more usual 7 minutes. Facsimile machines enable us to place written communications on desks instantly. We have come to expect, and in many cases receive, instant gratification of our wants and needs.

This same instant gratification has spilled over into the area of service delivery. Thanks to advancing computer technology in the business world, clients can have instant access to a staggering array of information and services. In many instances, instant access is the norm. This creates intense pressure on those of us who provide client services. Our clients have low tolerance for slow responses. Telephones must be answered promptly; telephone calls must be returned as soon as possible. Appointments must be scheduled and kept sooner rather than later.

To exacerbate the pressure to provide prompt, timely service, telecommunication technology has given us the tools to keep in touch wherever we may travel. As this material is being written, a cellular network is promoting its full line of communications tools: cellular phones, pagers and airfones to complement its well known telephone system. One particular promotion ends with the line: "Now there's no excuse for not keeping in touch — unless you don't want to." On hearing this comment, clients can only conclude that the reason you have not returned their calls is that you don't want to.

Clearly, it is more important than ever before to ensure that your clients receive timely service. This includes each client contact from telephone calls to written correspondence and reports. Time frames should be established for those services that cannot be provided promptly. Once set, you should make every effort possible to ensure that the deadlines are kept.

In setting priorities and establishing deadlines you should practice the principles of effective time management. Important and urgent matters always receive top priority. Although filing income tax returns is always important, the task does not become urgent until April. Next in priority come matters that must be dealt with urgently. These generally require some form of crisis management as a preliminary step to final resolution. Lastly are those matters that are important but not yet urgent. Left unattended, these matters have the tendency to become important and urgent.

It is well to remember that timeliness does not always mean instant service. In each case, you and your client should come to a common understanding of what timeliness means.

Add Value To Standard Services

The best method of distinguishing your standardized services from those of your competitors is to add something of value. Added value could take the form of additional service or information. For example, automobile manufacturers add value to the purchase of a new car by providing roadside assistance plans. Similarly, drug stores record the history of their customers' prescriptions and use this record to provide health advice and safeguards. The nature of the value that you add to your service depends upon your own resources and creativity.

The following table is intended as a starting point in identifying opportunities to add value to your own services.

Typical Service	Standard Service	Value Added Service
Accounting/ Bookkeeping	Preparing financial records and statements	Advising on increasing revenue, decreasing costs
Analyzing Investments	Identifying strengths, weaknesses of investments	Clarifying personal financial goals
Computer Programming	Preparing unique computer programs	Advising on related packaged software
Desk-Top Publishing	Preparing camera ready material for printing	Recommending reliable artist for custom artwork
Editing	Correcting/ improving written copy	Suggesting suitable layout and design
Management Consulting	Assisting to improve management effectiveness	Suggesting new marketing opportunities
Newsletter Publishing	Publishing and distributing newsletters	Recommending additional sources of information
Selling products	Distributing products	Ensuring customer knows benefits of the product
Training	Training others in personal or business skills	Recommending sources of advanced training
Typing	Preparing reports and documents	Editing for and correcting spelling/ grammar

For maximum effectiveness, these value added services should meet the following three criteria:

Brief: They should be brief, supplemental services to your clients. They should not overshadow your standard services.

Accurate: Providing wrong or misleading advice or recommendations not only negates the value added service but reduces the credibility of your standard services as well.

Relevant: Your value added services must be relevant to your client and his or her situation; again, an awareness of client needs is essential.

12 WHAT YOU NEED TO START YOUR HOME BUSINESS

Success in your home business depends to a large degree upon the preparation or homework that you do before you start. This chapter deals with your business or organizational needs. As noted, Chapter 16 deals with client needs.

Awareness of Clients' Needs

Successful businesses are client-driven. This means your business must be based on your ability to meet other people's needs, not on your own skills and resources, regardless of how impressive they might be. Before starting to plan your business, you must satisfy yourself that there are specific needs in the marketplace that you can meet. Once you have done this, identify resources that you have or can acquire that you will use in meeting these needs. Step One in the preparation of your marketing plan in Chapter 16 will help with this process.

Your Needs

Once you have identified what your clients need from you, and satisfied yourself that you can meet this need, you must determine what you will require to operate your business. The following checklist outlines some standard requirements.

Start-up Check-List

In the first column indicate whether or not you need the item. In the second column, estimate the initial or one-time start-up cost of the item. In the third column, estimate ongoing monthly expenses. The checklist will be easier to use if you enlarge it to letter size, using a photocopier with enlarging capabilities.

ITEM	REQ'D	START-UP COST	MONTHLY COST
Business Plan			
Business Name			
Office Area			
Office Furniture			
Office Equipment: telephone			
answering machine			
computer			
printer			
fax machine			
copier			
cellular phone			
pager			
line manager			
modem			
Specialized Equipment			
Office Supplies			
Computer Software: wordprocessing			
spreadsheet			
accounting			
contact/client data base			
project management			
desktop publishing			
CAD			
other			
Stationery: business cards			
letterhead			
envelopes			
other			
Automobile			
Licences, permits, etc.			
Tax registrations: Sales Tax			
Income Tax			
other			
Membership Fees			
Insurance: Business			
Liability			
Life			
Disability			
Banking Services: Chequing Account			
Line of Credit			
Credit Card			
Other:			
Professional Advice: Accountant			
Lawyer			
Other			
TOTALS			

By adding the second and third columns respectively, you can estimate your initial or start-up costs and your monthly operating expenses. These figures will be used in preparing your business plan, outlined in Chapter 14.

Business Plan

Although many businesses try, few will succeed in the long run without a business plan. Your plan will determine your goals and identify the strategies that you will follow in achieving them. The development of a business plan is set out in further detail below in Chapter 14.

Business Name

As a rule, if you carry on business in a name other than your own, you must register the name with an appropriate government department. Registration is usually a very simple process. You can and should do it yourself.

In choosing a name for your business, you should choose a name that accurately reflects your services. This will assist you in your marketing activities.

It may be advantageous for you to incorporate your business. In addition to limiting your personal liability, there are a number of tax advantages to incorporation. These advantages include reduced income tax on the corporation and a greater potential for income splitting between you and your spouse. You should discuss these possible advantages with your accountant. If you do incorporate, you can do this work yourself. There are many books and publications available that will help you. Among the best is the series of incorporation guides published by Self Counsel Press, available in most book stores and many libraries.

Office Area

The best home office space is the space that works best for you. Some people, like me, prefer working in basement offices. Others prefer second floor locations in spare rooms, while others opt for custom designed facilities over garages or attached to their houses. It's your choice — select the office space that you think will be comfortable for you and acceptable to other members of the household.

If used primarily for business purposes, your home office space becomes a tax deductible expense. Simply calculate the percentage of the total floor space of your house that your office occupies. This percentage of house occupancy costs — taxes, utilities, maintenance — becomes a tax deductible expense. Check with your accountant or tax advisor for further clarification.

Office Furniture

You do not need designer furniture or even new furniture for your home office. Again the choice is up to you. Whatever works best for you is the best furniture for your home office. As a bare minimum, you will need a desk, a chair and a filing cabinet. Beyond that, it's whatever furniture meets your needs, wants and budget.

Office Equipment:

Telephone   Although it can be done, using your home telephone line is not recommended. You should have a touch tone line dedicated to business use. It is, however, a good idea to have two or three two-line telephones in addition to the one in your office. This will allow you to take business calls when you are away from your desk, in other parts of the house. If available, you should also have call waiting. Clients hate busy signals. An added bonus of having additional two line telephones is increased house-hold peace. Having two telephone lines, each with call waiting, has allowed our two teenage daughters unlimited telephone time — apparently a must for teenagers — without their fighting and our missing a call. The best part is that your telephone line is tax deductible. When lining up your telephone service, make arrangements for a telephone credit card. This will enable you to charge long distance calls to your business number. Be sure to keep your card number confidential.

Since proper identification is not necessary to use it, anyone who has the number can make long distance calls and charge them to your business number.

Answering machine   You should not try to operate your home business without one. Technological advances have resulted in very low cost effective answering machines. Many telephones and fax machines have them built-in. Required features include voice activated message taking and remote access for listening to your messages and for changing out-going messages.

Computer   A computer is as essential to your home business as is a telephone. This will enable you to attend to client needs and administrative needs without the necessity of purchasing secretarial and clerical services. The choice of computer is virtually limitless. If buying a new system, you should have a minimum of 40 MB of hard disk memory and 4 MB of RAM. The rest of the bells and whistles, including laptops and portables, is up to you. If you are a "technopeasant", as I was when I started my home business, take some basic courses to learn about computer operation and keyboarding — typing on the computer keyboard. It is a small expenditure of time and money but well worth the effort.

Printer   If your business will involve the preparation of reports and other written material, you should invest in a laser printer. Otherwise a good quality dot matrix printer will provide you with adequate service. As with all computer equipment, make the purchasing decision on the basis of what you need rather than what the sales representative has to sell.

Fax Machine   There are three optional approaches to the use of a fax machine. One is the standard fax machine with a dedicated telephone line. Unless you use the line manager referred to below, this will require a separate dedicated telephone line. Without a line manager, a stand alone fax machine is not recommended. Second is the combination of fax machine and answering machine. Newer models have a built-in silicone chip that distinguishes incoming telephone calls as being either fax or telephone and routes the call accordingly. This approach is very popular with home business operators, most of whom report that the system works exceptionally well. A third approach is to have a fax card installed in your computer and attached to a modem. This will enable you to use your computer terminal to send and receive fax messages. This technique works especially well if all of the faxes that you send are computer generated.

Copier   If you anticipate the need for making many copies of reports and correspondence, you might consider purchasing a photocopier for use in your home office. There are many small and relatively inexpensive copiers designed for home use. The alternative to having a home copier is to make regular trips to quick print shops. You can also have copies made in many office supply stores, drug stores, libraries and so forth. If you are making a large number of copies of relatively few documents, it is best to have the copying done in a quick print shop.

Cellular Telephone   Unless you plan to make and receive a large number of telephone calls away from your office, a cellular phone is not absolutely essential. Before committing yourself to such a phone, track the number of calls you make away from your office and record the accessability to public phones. Although I have a phone in my car, I am amazed at how often I use alternatives — primarily public phones and telephones in client reception areas. With remote access to my answering machine, I can use these alternatives to check for messages when and where convenient, without using my car phone.

If you do choose to have a cellular telephone, purchase a totally portable model. This will enable you to carry the phone with you if you travel in a different vehicle and allow you to use your own phone away from your car.

Pager   Unless it is important that your callers have instant access to you, a pager is not necessary. With an answering machine that you check regularly for messages you can keep in touch with your callers without the expense and sense of urgency that are features of pagers.

Line Manager   This is a device that fits onto your telephone line that directs incoming telephone calls to their appropriate destinations: telephone, answering machine, fax, or computer modem. This is a must if you use more than one piece of equipment connected to your telephone line.

Modem   If you exchange computer data with anyone else, you will require a modem. If you use a computer modem, you must also have and use anti-virus software.

Specialized Equipment

Different businesses require different equipment. If your business generates a great deal of mail, you will probably want a postage meter. If you will be collating and stapling batches of printed material, you might need collating equipment and an electric stapler. If you need specialized equipment, you will know what you need. Don't forget to include it in your planning. If you don't need specialized equipment, simply mark "no" on the checklist and move on.

Office Supplies

Office supplies include everything from pens, pencils and paper to pins, tape and paper clips. You probably won't need too much of any one thing so don't buy in large quantities until you know the volume that you will be using.

Computer Software

The viability of home businesses has arisen in large part due to the increasing availability of inexpensive and effective computer technology. Projects that formerly required sophisticated computer facilities housed in costly office premises can now be effectively and efficiently completed by home businesses. In addition to the broad range of affordable and readily available software, the following can assist you in the administration and management of your business.

Wordprocessing   With appropriate word processing software, you need never again depend upon a secretary to complete your paper work. Regardless of the program that you select, make sure that it has spell check and grammar check capabilities.

Spreadsheet   The calculations outlined in the next chapter are a breeze with a simple spread sheet program. You would be amazed at the versatility and usefulness of spread-sheet applications in home business operations. These uses include cash flow forecasting and simple data analysis. If you start your business without a spreadsheet application, it will be only a matter of time before you realize that you need one.

Accounting   Like it or not, you are going to have to keep track of your revenues and expenses. Many accounting packages include cheque writing features and produce financial reports on a regular basis. If you have a computer, there is no reason for maintaining your financial records manually.

Contact/Client Data Base   This program will allow you to track contacts with all of your clients, potential clients and contacts. Most will also allow you undertake mass mailings. For a very small initial investment, you will have a very powerful marketing tool.

Desktop Publishing   Unless you are planning on producing a large volume of print communications yourself, this is not an essential program. For newsletters and presentations, most wordprocessing programs will provide adequate quality.

Other   If you like playing with computers there is no end to the range of additional software that you can buy. If however, you see computers as business tools and not leisure activities, you do not need much more than what is outlined above.

Stationery

Your paper wardrobe — your stationery — is one of your most important marketing tools. Since it is unlikely that your clients and potential clients will be seeing your office, your stationery must present the image of competence and professionalism. The time and effort involved in designing good stationery will be returned several times over. Take the time and spend the money to get the best stationery that you can afford. In selecting paper, look for recycled paper — excellent quality recycled paper stock is available. (This book is printed on recycled paper).

Automobile

If you use your automobile to travel from your place of business (your home) to your clients' places of business, your related automobile expenses will be tax deductions. Unless you use your automobile exclusively for business, only a portion of automobile expenses will be tax deductible. Check with your accountant.

Licences, permits, etc.

As a rule, you do not need a licence or permit to operate a business from your home. Some businesses — hairdressing, medical or dental services etc — do, however, require licensing. Make sure that, if you require a licence, you get it before you start your business.

Tax registrations

If you will be collecting taxes from your clients you must register with the appropriate tax authorities. Check with your local tax offices to determine the registration procedure.

Membership Fees

These include fees for membership in professional and trade associations as well as business and local associations. Before including a membership fee as a business expense, check with your accountant to ensure that the membership fee does in fact qualify as a deductible business expense.

Insurance:

Property   Although it is unlikely that you will require special insurance for your home business, you should check with your agent or broker to ensure that your current property insurance will cover your business assets. You might also enquire as to whether or not you can purchase business interruption insurance. This would cover the costs involved should the operation of your business be interrupted by major property damage to your home.

Liability   If available and reasonably priced, you might consider liability insurance if there is any risk of your clients suffering a loss as a result of your services. If liability insurance is either not available or too costly, you can limit your personal liability by incorporating your business.

Life   Although not likely to be considered a business expense, life insurance remains an important component of your business operation. Term insurance rather than whole life is probably best. The premiums can be paid by the business and charged back to you personally.

Disability   Like life insurance, this is not usually a business expense, although the premiums can be paid by the business and charged back to you. It is, however, important that you have adequate coverage to protect your income in the event of illness or disability.

Banking Services

Your banker can be your best friend as you start your own business. It is however important that you select a banker whom you like and who understands your business activities. Many entrepreneurs use different banks for their business and personal banking. They believe that this prevents the bank from gaining too strong a hold over them. You will need some or all of the following banking services.

Chequing Account These come in many forms and are known by many names. Make sure that you understand the features of the account you select including the service charges to be levied.

Line of Credit This is a form of a loan, designed to cover the period between completing work for your client and receiving payment for the work. Many a business has been saved by a line of credit. Again, make sure that you understand the costs involved.

Credit Card Some banks and financial institutions offer credit cards in the business name; others will issue the cards only in your personal name. The bewildering array of options available make it difficult to make the most appropriate choice. Some form of credit card is, however, a must for business operations.

Other Today's banks offer a broad range of other services to business clients. Some of these services might be exactly the services that you require. As with all banking activities, make sure that you understand what you are getting and how much you are paying it.

Professional Advice

Accountant With good accounting or book-keeping software you will not need a book-keeper or accountant. Your system can prepare all the statements that you need. You might, however, need an accountant to interpret the statements, or provide you with tax advice and prepare your tax returns. If you decide that you want or need an accountant, you don't necessarily need one with a professional designation such as Certified Public Accountant or Chartered Accountant. Many individuals who call themselves accountants can provide you with the same quality of financial and tax advice at a much lower cost. As with banking, make sure that you understand what you are getting from your accountant and how much you are paying for it.

Lawyer   As noted above, you can do many things without a lawyer. There are, however, times when you must consult a lawyer. These situations would include clarification as to the applicability of specific laws, regulations or municipal bylaws to your business, alleged violation of any statutes, and commencement or defence of court actions. Lawyers are experiencing difficult times and many are eager for work. Shop around for the lawyer who will provide you with the services that you need at a price you are willing to pay. The fierce competition in the profession should make it possible for you to have an initial consultation with a lawyer at no charge.

Other

Just as no two individuals are alike, no two home businesses are alike. Some people can start their businesses without any decorating or structural changes to their homes while others will require renovations or additions. Some business people might need marketing help while others might require computer assistance. Before leaving the start-up check-list make sure that you have added any special needs that you might have.

13 FINANCIAL FORECASTING

F inancial forecasting is an essential ingredient of planning your home business. Your forecasts will provide you with a good indication of the revenue that you must produce to cover your operating expenses.

Projecting Operating Overhead

Projecting revenue for the first time is the most difficult aspect of financial forecasting. Your projections will be based on such factors as how much you charge for your services and what volume of revenue your total services will yield. Unless your past experience enables you to determine your fees and estimate your fee revenue, your financial projections will be based on a limited amount of reliable information. In this case, the best approach is work from what is known to what is not known. Thus, before addressing revenue projections, which are difficult to determine for the first time, it is best to first calculate monthly overhead amounts, which are easily identified. Having determined the monthly overhead, it is a simple task to project revenue to meet or exceed these overhead figures.

Typical Expenses

The following list details typical expense items. It is not likely that all of them will apply to you and your business. Conversely, it is possible that your business will have expense items that are not included in this list. As was the case with start-up expenses, customize this list to meet your own needs.

You can use your spreadsheet program to calculate the overhead amounts. Amounts for individual items can be based on estimates provided by suppliers, or alternatively, estimated as a percentage of total expenses. The second column lists appropriate percentages, based on the experience of others.

Expense Item	% of Total Expense	Monthly	Annual
Accounting & Legal	1.8		
Automobile	5.9		
Clerical Support†	17.8		
Dues & Subscriptions	1.3		
Insurance	0.4		
Licenses & Taxes	0.3		
Management‡	12.1		
Marketing	41.8		
Other	3.1		
Printing & Copying	2.1		
Professional Development	5.6		
Stationery & Office Supplies	0.4		
Telephone & Postage	7.2		
Totals	**100.0**		

† This would include secretarial and clerical services purchased from outside sources.
‡ This represents ths cost of your time spent in managing your business.

On average, you will have 20 working days per month. Thus your **daily overhead** equals your monthly overhead divided by 20.

Fee Revenue

Obviously, if you are to survive in the long run, your fee revenue must at least equal your overhead. Your profit will come from revenue that remains after your overhead has been paid.

In the absence of more reliable information, the best means of estimating your profit is to set a specific income goal. This income goal should be determined after consideration of both past income and your personal financial needs.

Allowing for two weeks of holidays, weekends off and 10 statutory holidays, you will have 240 working days per year. By dividing your income goal by 240, you will determine your rate of income per day. By combining this figure with the daily overhead amount as determined above, you will have identified the amount of income that you must generate daily to achieve your personal income goal and meet your overhead. This amount should be your daily billing rate. The calculation is set out below:

1. Annual Income goal   _____
2. Income Per Day (Income goal/240)   _____
3. Daily Overhead Rate   _____
   Daily Billing Rate:
   Add lines 2 & 3   _____

Using an 8 hour day as a standard working day, your hourly rate is calculated as being 1/8 of your daily billing rate.

The next step in forecasting your revenue is to estimate the number of hours for which you will be able to bill clients and collect the fees. Operating your own business, virtually alone, will create unprecedented demands on your time. In addition to providing services to your clients, you must devote time to marketing and selling activities (typically 20% of your time), to managing your business (about 10% of your time), and to professional development activities (about 5% of your time). Not allowing yourself any time for sickness, you will have 65% of your time, 156 days or 1300 hours available for client service.

Using these estimates, calculating annual fee revenue is simple:

Hourly rate X 1300 hours = annual fee revenue.

You now have the necessary information to forecast your fees and expenses for your first year of operation. Although you could divide these numbers by 12 to determine your average monthly revenue and expenses, these figures being averages, are of little assistance for planning purposes. The next step is to prepare a cash flow forecast, as outlined in the next section.

Cash Flow Forecast

As its name suggests, a cash flow forecast is a forecast of cash flow — cash flowing into and out of your business. The forecast is based on your predictions of when you expect to receive payment of your fees from your clients and when you expect to make payments to your suppliers and to yourself.

In preparing your cash flow forecast, you should consider the following factors.

Revenue

- regardless of the payment provisions on your invoices, most clients will pay 30-60 days after they have been invoiced
- some clients, especially government, will pay you more than 60 days after invoice date
- some clients will not pay you at all
- until you have established a significant profile and clients come to you instead of vice versa, few clients will pay you anything in advance

Expenses

- some of your suppliers will demand pre-payment
- most of your suppliers will demand payment in 30 days or less

Completing your cash flow forecast is another exercise that is easier with the use of a computer spread sheet. If you plan to complete the forecast manually, enlarge both charts to letter size and make several copies using a photocopier with enlarging capability. You could also prepare your own customized form using your own descriptions of your cash receipts and revenues. Make a number of photocopies of the form and complete it using your calculator, pencil and eraser. If nothing else, this exercise will convince you of the need for a spread sheet program on your computer.

Typical Cash Disbursement Forecast For First 12 Month Period

Month	1	2	3	4	5	6	7	8	9	10	11	12
Accounting & Legal												
Automobile												
Clerical Support†												
Dues & Subscriptions												
Insurance												
Licenses & Taxes												
Management‡												
Marketing												
Other												
Printing & Copying												
Professional Development												
Stationery & Office Supplies												
Telephone & Postage												
TOTAL DISBURSEMENTS												

† This would include secretarial and clerical services purchased from outside sources.
‡ This represents ths cost of your time spent in managing your business.

Typical Cash Flow Forecast For First 12 Month Period

Month	1	2	3	4	5	6	7	8	9	10	11	12
CASH RECEIPTS: Fee Revenue												
Other Revenue												
TOTAL REVENUE												
TOTAL DISBURSEMENTS (from previous chart)												
NET CASH FLOW												
CUMULATIVE CASH FLOW												

You prepare your cash flow forecast using as much detail as you believe appropriate.

Cash Receipts These are to be recorded in the month in which you expect to receive payment.

Fee Revenue This is not likely to be equal for the entire 12 months. Record where you anticipate having high fee revenue and low fee revenue.

Other Revenue This could include your own cash contributions and revenue from other sources.

Cash Disbursements These are to be recorded in the months in which you anticipate making actual payment. For improved management information, you should classify each of the expense categories into sub-categories.

Accounting & Legal Normally, your accounting expenses are high around tax time. Barring unforseen problems, your legal expenses will be high only at start-up.

Automobile Total projected operating expenses can be averaged over 12 months.

Clerical Support These expenses, usually low in slow times, will be higher when you anticipate larger projects.

Dues & Subscriptions Membership dues are usually paid annually; subscriptions may be paid at more frequent intervals. This category should be sub-divided.

Insurance Although insurance premiums are normally billed annually, many companies will provide interim or instalment billing.

Licenses & Taxes These are usually paid on an instalment basis.

Management
Marketing
Other
Printing & Copying
} Monthly Averages can be used for these items.

Professional Development If you know when specific courses and training will be taken, you can record in the appropriate months.

Stationery & Office Supplies } Monthly Averages can
Telephone & Postage } be used for these items.

Personal Draw This represents the compensation that you will receive for managing the business and delivering services to your clients. To ensure that the business maintains a strong cash flow, you should set the amount of the draw at a level that covers what you require for household and personal expenses. You should receive your personal draw on a regular basis. As the business begins to show a profit, you can pay yourself a bonus from any accumulated cash surplus.

Projected Income Statements

These statements project revenue by quarter over a period of 1-2 years. In summarizing the cash flow forecasts, they provide you with projections as to what income you can expect if your business develops as planned. You can classify the operating expenses into whatever categories will be meaningful to you. The following form will assist you in preparing the statements.

PROJECTED INCOME STATEMENT

	First Quarter	Second Quarter	Third Quarter	Fourth Quarter	Total Year 1	Total Year 2
Fee Revenue						
Less: Expenses Operating						
Marketing						
Other						
Operating Profit						
Less: Your Draw						
NET INCOME						

14 YOUR BUSINESS PLAN

Unless you enjoy the challenge of discovering new territories without any kind of assistance, you are not likely to try to reach an unfamiliar destination without a road map. By using a road map, you can minimize the risks of getting lost.

Similarly by using a business plan, you can minimize the risks of losing time and money usually associated with starting a new business venture. Uniform road maps are readily available from a wide variety of sources. Business plans, on the other hand, are neither uniform nor readily available. You must prepare your own plan, reflecting your own unique characteristics and those of your business. In preparing your business plan, you should be as specific as possible to provide a sense of direction for your business for the coming year. You must also provide enough flexibility to enable you to respond to new and unexpected opportunities as they arise.

As well as providing you with a requisite sense of direction, a well prepared business plan will assist you in your dealings with your bank and other sources of financing.

Developing Your Plan

The following material outlines the details that are usually found in business plans. In working with this material, you should consider only those elements that are relevant to your specific business. Although the material is as complete as possible, it may well be that there are issues relevant to your business that are not addressed. You should incorporate your consideration of these issues into your business plan.

Objectives: Your objectives will describe in detail what service you will provide. They could reflect the image that you want to project to your clients. They might also reflect the market or niche market in which you plan to specialize and the type of client base you would like to build. In their finished form, your objectives should read like the copy for a well prepared 30 second commercial: clear, concise and complete.

Competition: A thorough analysis of your competition is essential. This analysis will include answering the following questions:
• who are your competitors?
• where are they located?
• how long have they been in business?
• how do they price their services?
• who are their major clients?
• what are their unique strengths?
• what are their unique weaknesses?
• what can they do better than I can?
• what can I do better then they can?

You can gather the information necessary for this analysis from your own knowledge of the competition, from suppliers, clients, colleagues, third parties or anyone with solid information about your competition. When asking for information, only ask for information that you are certain that the person you are asking can provide. If you ask for information that he or she can't provide, you risk straining the relationship.

When reviewing information, consider its source. Is the information realistic and believable? Is the source of the information believable and credible? Is the information intended to be deceptive or to mislead you? Once you have analyzed the information, you can develop a profile of your competitors that will enable you to differentiate your business from theirs. The profile will also enable you to project why clients will prefer your services over those of your competitors. A written summary of your analysis will form part of your business plan.

Clients: Defining your client base is addressed in detail in the following chapter. For purposes of your business plan, you should prepare a brief summary describing your clients and their needs that you will be meeting.

Pricing Your Services: The preceding chapter outlines how to determine the prices to charge for your services. For purposes of your business plan, include a brief summary covering:
- hourly and daily rate;
- average fees per project;
- projected total fees;
- break-even point — level of sales to just cover operating expenses;
- how your prices compare to the competition.

Operating Requirements: This section of the business plan identifies the licences, permits and resources that you will require to begin and maintain your business operations. Included in these requirements are:
- compliance with federal, provincial or state and municipal government regulations;
- obtaining the necessary permits and licences to carry on your specific business;
- registration for the collection of sales tax, if applicable;
- acquisition of major pieces of equipment and furniture;
- skills required to provide services to clients, and source and cost of acquiring these skills;
- if dealing with third party financing, i.e. banks or private investors, an outline of your own relevant skills and experience;

Financial Considerations

Start-up, Cash Flow Forecast and Projected Income Statements

The preceding chapter outlines how you can prepare these statements. Once they are in their final form, you should incorporate copies into your business plan.

Using Your Plan

Once prepared, your business plan should not be consigned to your business archives. Just as you use a road map to monitor your progress toward your destination, you should use your plan to monitor progress towards your ultimate business goals. If your business is developing as planned, you can proceed confident in the knowledge that if you stay the course you will achieve your overall goals. Conversely, if things are not developing as planned, you can make mid-course corrections that will enable you to modify your goals so that they more accurately reflect your operating experience. Your business plan can and will serve as an effective road map for you; you must, however, consult it regularly. It will be of little use filed in the bottom drawer of your desk.

15 HOW TO MARKET YOUR HOME BUSINESS

The concept of marketing is relatively new to the business world. It arose in the mid-1950's to challenge the approaches that manufacturers followed in getting their goods into the hands of the ultimate consumers.

One such approach — **the production concept** — holds that consumers will favour those products that are widely available and low in cost. Managers of production oriented organizations concentrate on achieving high production efficiency and wide distribution coverage. Ford Motor Company, for example, put all of its resources into perfecting the mass production of standardized automobiles to bring down their costs so that ordinary consumers could afford them. Standardization is no longer acceptable to today's consumers. They look for products and services that meet their own unique needs.

Another — **the product concept** — holds that consumers will favour those products that offer the most quality, performance, and features. Managers in these product oriented organizations focus on making good products and improving them over time. This concept gives rise to the cliche: *build a better mouse-trap and the world will beat a path to your door.* Experience has taught us that this is not always true. Just because you may have a better mouse trap doesn't mean that it will sell. What makes it better than the others? How will the world know about the mouse trap or even that it is better? How will the world know where to find the mouse trap? Does the world really need another mouse trap? These are just a few of the questions that arise to challenge the validity of the product concept.

A third approach — **the selling or sales concept** — holds that consumers, if left alone, will ordinarily not buy enough of the organization's products. The organization must undertake aggressive selling and promotion effort. Selling is often supported by extensive advertising and promotional campaigns. Closing the sale becomes more important than the product or service and the customer. As a result, many consumers believe that marketing is advertising and hard selling.

Peter Drucker, a leading management expert has commented:

"There will always, one can assume, be need for some selling. But the aim of marketing is to make selling superfluous. **The aim of marketing is to know and understand the customer so well that the product or service fits him and sells itself** [Emphasis Added]. Ideally, marketing should result in a customer who is ready to buy. All that should be needed then is to make the product or service available.[12]

The marketing concept indicates that the key to achieving your business goals consists of determining the needs and expectations of your clients and meeting them more effectively and efficiently than your competitors.

Non-technical ways of expressing this approach include: "Find needs and fill them" and "make what will sell, don't try to sell what you can make."

Based on this approach, we can define **marketing** as **the process of identifying your clients' needs and expectations and using your resources to meet these needs and expectations.**

The Function of Marketing

Marketing has two very important purposes.

First and foremost, **it helps to protect and maintain your current client base**. Increasing competition in today's market place means that your clients are probably target clients for other businesses. For your business to continue to thrive in the long term, you must protect your client base from your competition. This can best be done by ensuring that you continue to meet your clients' needs on an on-going basis. Defensive marketing activities — maintaining regular contact with your clients, understanding your clients' shifting needs and demonstrating your responsiveness — will help protect your client base from erosion.

It is more efficient and more profitable to provide services to existing clients than to new ones. Less time is required to develop an understanding of the client and his or her needs; past dealings provide a wealth of useful information.

Second, **marketing activities generate new clients**. This new business consists of providing existing services to new clients. You are already able to deliver the service effectively and efficiently; only the clients are new.

An alternate source of new business would be to provide new services to new clients. Because the clients are new, you must identify their needs, wants and expectations. These may be different from the requirements of existing clients.

You cannot rely on existing relationships; you must establish your credibility and credentials with each new client before you can promote your new services.

There are two challenges — selling yourself and selling your service — to be met before the sale can be closed. Clearly, trying to sell new services to new clients is the most difficult approach to obtaining new business.

Developing Your Marketing Plan

Few marketing activities are likely to generate significant new business in the short term. Effective marketing involves the use of many strategies over a period of time. Because of this, a marketing plan is essential. It identifies your clients and their needs, clarifies your overall marketing goals and defines specific strategies. The following steps outline the development of your marketing plan.

Step One: Identify Your Clients and Their Needs

- who are your clients and target clients?
- what do they do? what business are they in?
- what is their sales volume? how many people do they employ? what fee will you receive from providing them with services?
- where are they located?
- what do they need from you today? what will they need from you in the future? what do they expect from you today? will they expect the same things in the future? if not, what will they expect?

Don't guess at the answers to questions addressing clients' needs. If you don't know the answers, find out. You can find out by asking your clients directly. If you have already done work for clients, the best means of identifying their future needs is by combining a client satisfaction interview, as outlined in Chapter 17, with some form of needs assessment. The needs assessment would focus on the trends that the clients see in their own industry and how these trends will impact on their operation. As you discuss the impact of these trends, you can discuss what services your clients anticipate requiring from you.

It may be necessary to do some secondary research in reference libraries or by asking others close to clients. Your network contacts identified in Chapter 18 can also be of immeasurable benefit.

Step Two: Match Your Resources to Your Clients' Needs

- what can you do now to meet your clients' needs?
- what additional resources — people, money, equipment skills etc — do you require now? in the future?
- what can you do better, faster, cheaper than your competition? how can you do this?
- what additional resources — people, money, equipment skills etc — do you require to maintain your competitive edge?

Be brutally honest with yourself in completing this assessment. You should identify your strengths and weaknesses and those of your competition to be sure that you are in fact the best person to serve your clients and potential clients. You should take steps to correct any weaknesses or improve any areas in which your competition is better than you.

Step Three: Marketing Communications

- how can you tell your clients and target clients that you can meet their needs better, faster, cheaper than your competition? How frequently will you have to do this?

Communications could include in-person meetings and interviews, speeches and formal presentations, personal letters and personalized mailings, newsletters, brochures, specialized hand-out material and advertising. Regardless of which communication tool that you use, you should be sure that they are the most appropriate vehicle for the people with whom you wish to communicate.

Step Four: Putting It All Together

- define your clients and target clients
- define the current and new services that you plan to deliver to each
- for new services, determine how you will acquire the necessary skills to deliver these services
- identify how you will communicate with clients and potential clients
- develop a time frame and budget for marketing communications

Once your plan has been prepared, it will serve as a blueprint as you market your services. The plan should be fairly general and flexible so that you can respond to new opportunities. Plans that are too rigid tend to be more of a handicap than a useful tool: they interfere with effective marketing and become obstacles to your success.

16 MARKETING STRATEGIES FOR YOUR HOME BUSINESS

To achieve your marketing goals, you must identify and follow appropriate marketing strategies. These strategies fall into one of two categories: **personal contact** and **planned communication**.

Effective Strategies

All of the strategies will help you keep in touch with existing clients, identify potential clients, and tell your existing and potential clients about your ability to meet their needs. In and of themselves, they are unlikely to bring new business to you. They will, however, help set up the opportunity for you to generate new business. *In the final analysis, it is your ability to sell both yourself and your services that will generate new business. To do this, you must deal with your clients and potential clients on a personal basis. You must also continually assure them that you understand and can help meet their specific needs.*

Personal Contact

The purpose of personal contact is to establish and maintain personal relationships with a broad range of individuals: clients, potential clients, referral and information sources etc. The most common approaches to establishing and maintaining these relationships are networking and participating in clubs and organizations.

Networking

This is the practice of establishing and maintaining

personal contact with a broad range of individuals including clients, potential clients, referral sources, information sources and "bird dogs", who point you in the direction of potential clients. It is one of the most effective marketing techniques available because it has many long term benefits. Properly practised, it is excellent for enhancing personal relationships with existing clients and developing new personal relationships with potential clients. Regular contact with members of your network also enables you to monitor new developments affecting your clients. This enables you to respond effectively to shifting client demands.

Advantages: Networking helps builds a third party sales force — your network contacts who promote you and your services and make referrals to you. As a result, it provides ongoing round-the-clock marketing. Your personal credibility with your network contacts provides you with a strong foundation for marketing and cross selling additional or new services. It is a subtle approach — you can sell yourself without being perceived as selling. Through your network contacts promoting you to their own network contacts, you can extend your reach and image beyond your immediate circle of friends and acquaintances.

Disadvantages: Effective networking is not necessarily easy. It requires discipline, an outgoing personality and a solid understanding of the selling process. It is also very time consuming to time consuming to establish and maintain. Fortunately there is excellent contact management software available to assist with the logistics of maintaining contact with your personal network. Networking seldom produces instant results; it is common for network contacts to generate new business, months and even years, after the initial contact was made.

General Comments: Networking is the basis of all successful businesses. It allows individuals to establish and maintain mutually beneficial relationships. It expedites the process of matching needs with the people and resources that can meet these needs. Establishing and maintaining your own network is vital to the success of your home business.

Membership In Clubs and Organizations

This strategy is a form of networking. It includes membership and participation in sports, social, community and charitable organizations. As a networking technique it is potentially effective. It does, however, require constant participation in the organization. Like all networking techniques, it yields long term benefits.

Advantages: Provided you are personally committed to the goals and objectives of the club or organization, your participation can be personally rewarding. Your participation will help to increase your personal profile and enable you to make contact with possible clients and potentially influential individuals. Once the initial contact has been made you can add these possible clients and potentially influential people to your personal network for future follow-up.

Disadvantages: The primary purpose of your participation in an organization should not be to further your marketing. Thus, your participation will provide little opportunity for direct marketing. The organization's activities should always take precedence over your marketing activities. Active marketing activities must take place outside of the organization's activities. It is possible that you may have competitors who belong to the same organization. This will limit your marketing potential.

General Comments: This approach will provide you with the opportunity to meet potential clients. You must, however, develop the relationship outside of the organization to ensure effective marketing. Your participation will not be effective if you join for business purposes only: other members will see your participation as a sham and be reluctant to deal with you. You must be committed to the goals of the organization and enjoy your participation.

Planned Communications

The purpose of planned communications is to present clear spoken or written messages about you, your credentials and expertise and your ability to assist clients. These messages are directed to specifically identified individuals or groups of individuals and are carefully planned and structured.

Speeches and Formal Presentations

These are prepared speeches and presentations to specifically identified groups. They are ideal opportunities to demonstrate your knowledge of a particular subject and can be used both to confirm your expertise in existing service areas and to introduce your expertise in new service areas. The benefits of these approaches are usually short term.

Advantages: In presenting yourself as an expert, each format can enhance your image. They are very flexible activities in which you can tailor the content of your message and your delivery style to meet the unique needs and expectations of the group you are addressing.

Disadvantages: For maximum effectiveness, these approaches depend upon good oral communication skills. They also require considerable preparation time and organized follow-up.

General Comments: Both approaches represent ideal formats for increasing your profile, enhancing your image, and demonstrating your expertise. You should obtain a list of people attending so that you can address their level of knowledge of your subject matter and conduct appropriate follow-up after the presentation. Follow-up with those people interested in you and your services is essential to ensure the effectiveness as a marketing tool. Unless you are a good speaker or are prepared to make the commitment to become a good speaker, you should not use this strategy.

Conducting Seminars and Workshops

Similar to speeches and presentations, these approaches involve more interaction between you as presenter and a smaller audience. They also represent very effective formats for demonstrating your expertise and knowledge of specific topics. The interactive format enables you to exchange information with members of your audience and for individual members of the audience to exchange information with each other. Short term benefits can be expected from seminars and workshops.

Advantages: As well as demonstrating your knowledge and expertise, these formats can demonstrate your personal skills and enable to you to develop relationships with individual participants. They are excellent vehicles for distributing printed material about you and your business. In workshop and seminar formats, it is also possible for you to deal with a large volume of complicated material by drawing on the collected knowledge and expertise of your audience. This in turn enables you to increase your own information and knowledge base.

Disadvantages: As a form of oral communication, these formats require well qualified and prepared speakers addressing current topics. To ensure their effectiveness, they also require considerable time to prepare and develop. Full marketing potential can only be realized through effective follow-up.

General Comments: The same comments made above regarding speeches and presentations apply to seminars and workshops. Being more interactive, these formats will enable you develop more personal relationships with individual participants. As well as good oral communication skills, effective group leadership skills are essential.

Print Communications

Included in this category are brochures, circulars, flyers,

and similar printed material prepared for general distribution. This format can be effectively used to communicate unique features of your business to clients and potential clients. Benefits will be long term.

Advantages: This technique can enhance your personal image and increase your profile, and that of your business, in your target market. These communication pieces can be professional sales vehicles.

Disadvantages: Print communications are sales tools only — you will still require personal involvement with clients or potential clients to obtain their business. To ensure effectiveness, there must be continuous distribution of your print communications. This could be a fairly serious problem as this format tends to be costly to develop, produce and maintain the currency of the materials.

General Comments: This approach is very effective when combined with oral communications. The print communication reinforces your spoken message and serves as a reminder of you and you presentation. With appropriate computer equipment you can produce some of these materials yourself.

Advertising

This is paid promotion of your business. Because you control the message, advertising is potentially very effective. However, the benefits will last only as long as the advertising continues.

Advantages: This is a vary flexible market approach: properly directed, you can target specific market segments. It can also be very effective in increasing the level of awareness of you and your business among clients and potential clients. Advertising will help you to promote your existing services as well as your new services. Through advertising, you can reach large potentially large audience.

Disadvantages: Advertising is not appropriate for all businesses. It can also be very expensive for the results that you achieve. To reach your target, your advertising must compete with large number of commercial messages from other advertisers.

General Comments: There is a wide range of advertising media available. These include print and electronic media, billboards, transit advertising and so forth. This broad choice enables you to select the appropriate advertising vehicle to reach your target audience. Note that advertising will be effective for generating new leads only. It is not likely to generate business in and of itself.

Direct Mail

This approach involves mailing specific information to individually identified contacts. Newsletters are currently a popular form of direct mail. This technique is a very effective means of communicating with individual contacts. It is also good for keeping in touch all of your network contacts: existing clients, potential clients, personal contacts and referral sources.

Advantages: This is a relatively low cost technique, especially when using appropriate computer programs. mailings can be customized for each type of contact, client or potential client. Is very effective in yielding prospects;

Disadvantages: To realize maximum benefits you will require a versatile computer program to ensure properly targeted mailings and effective follow-up. Direct mailings are obvious selling tactics. As such, your mailings must compete with the growing number of direct mailings to business people. Direct mail also results in a very low response rate: you can consider your mailing successful if you realize a 1% return rate.

General Comments: This can be a very effective communication tool. For best results, you should avoid using mailing labels and print directly onto the envelopes. Experience has also shown that the use of postage stamps rather than postage meters increases the effectiveness of the mailing. Without effective follow-up, direct mail is unlikely to yield worthwhile results.

Writing for Publication

This includes preparing written articles for publication in journals, magazines, newsletters, newspapers etc. published by others. Also included is writing books for publication by others or yourself. This is an excellent approach for increasing your personal profile and professional credibility. It also enables you to demonstrate your specialized knowledge and expertise.

Advantages: Through writing you can provide useful information to clients and to potential clients. You can also maintain a long lasting presence. Reprints of your writing can be used as additional marketing tools.

Disadvantages: good writing requires a considerable time commitment to properly research and prepare the material. It is often difficult to have material published by others; self publishing is a very onerous task.

General Comments: This is another excellent strategy for establishing your credentials. It is, however, neither fast nor easy.

Public Relations

As opposed to advertising, this is involves using the media to generate free publicity for you and your business. If you can arrange it, good public relations is probably the best marketing technique available.

Advantages: Comments by third parties, especially in the media, are thought to be more objective and hence more credible. Because the third parties are not usually paid to endorse, public relations can be inexpensive.

Disadvantages: Free publicity doesn't just happen; it takes considerable time and effort. To attract attention of media people — editors, reporters, writers, columnists etc. your information must be newsworthy and interesting to readers. It must compete for space with numerous other equally interesting articles.

General Comments: Unless you are well connected to media people, your best approach to media relations is to hire a public relations specialist whose job it is to create publicity for you.

Ineffective Strategies

Cold Calls

Sometimes the only way to go **but**

- they are obvious selling
- they are inefficient
- few people like to do them.

Telemarketing

Sometimes they can provide a sampling of the interest or needs in a given market segment **but**

- they are obvious selling
- they are inefficient
- few people like to make the calls
- few people like to receive the calls.

17 MEASURING CLIENT SATISFACTION

Client satisfaction can be measured by a number of methods. Figure 17-1 outlines different approaches that might be used.

Figure 17-1
Methods of Measuring Client Satisfaction

Informal	Formal
ask client contact	interview client contact
ask client employees	interview client contact and decision makers
ask client's other advisors e.g. lawyer, accountant etc.	evaluation on completion of of work as in Figure 8-2
ask client's customers or clients	client satisfaction survey as in Figures 8-3 to 8-5

Informal Techniques

This approach involves simply checking on the client's satisfaction at appropriate stages. Anyone involved in the client work can be asked for feedback. Table 17-1 lists typical individuals who might be asked for feedback.

Use the following guidelines in asking for feedback:

Be very selective in asking for feedback.

Asking for feedback too often or of too many people suggests insecurity or lack of confidence. It is better to ask for feedback too seldom than too frequently.

Make clear that your request for feedback pertains to your services only.

Soliciting feedback for the purpose of gathering additional information about your client could seriously jeopardize your relationship with your client.

Obtain your client's approval before speaking to other employees, advisors or customers.

Provided your request is framed in terms of "I would like to speak to... about the effectiveness of my services and how they can be improved", your client will probably approve of your plans. Otherwise, your client may perceive you to be trying to work behind his or her back.

Ensure that your request is specific and focused.

A vague question like "how am I doing?" will no doubt be answered with an equally vague "not too bad". Use the questions contained in Figures 17-2 to frame your questions.

You could also ask the following questions:

1. What am I doing that I should continue to do?
2. What am I doing that I should stop doing?
3. What am I not doing that I should start doing?

This will enable you to focus on specific issues and make whatever changes you and your client believe appropriate.

On receiving feedback, limit changes or modifications to those necessary to ensure the client's immediate satisfaction. Unless absolutely essential, do not attempt a major overhaul as a mid-course correction. There is a significant difference between using client feedback to satisfy an individual client and using feedback to plan overall improvements. It is only after the immediate needs of clients have been attended to that consideration can be given to changes in practices and policies.

Valuable as it is, the informal approach to measuring client satisfaction has its limitations. Like a single snapshot, it provides a view pertaining to one client matter at a specific point in time. It does not indicate whether the satisfaction has increased or decreased over time; unless the client is specifically asked, there will be no identification of opportunities for improvement.

Formal Techniques

It is usually more effective to measure client satisfaction through a more formal structured approach. One such format involves interviews between you and representatives of your client. The material contained in Figure 17-2 could be used in an interview format. These interviews, conducted either by telephone or in person, can address a wide range of topics. The interviews also allow direct interaction between you and your clients. They also provide your clients with the opportunity of expanding on specific answers and providing additional information. A further advantage of interviews is that they often enable you to identify additional unmet client needs. Having identified these needs, you are well positioned to demonstrate to the client how well you can help meet these needs. Clearly evaluation interviews can be very effective marketing techniques.

The interview process is however, extremely time consuming. It is often difficult to schedule these interviews on a timely basis.

The most cost-effective means of measuring client satisfaction is a formal client survey. Such an approach requires surveying your clients at fixed points in time. An ideal time to measure client satisfaction is immediately after you have completed the work. Another would be a significant dates for clients such fiscal year ends or completion of routine reports. Figure 17-2 is a sample of a client satisfaction questionnaire.

Figure 17-2
How Did I Do?
(for use on completion of work)

I am committed to constantly improving the quality of my services to clients. Feedback from clients is an important component of this process.

I would appreciate your taking a few minutes to complete this brief questionnaire to provide me with your feedback. Please feel free to add appropriate comments.

1. Services provided _____.

2. Why did you select my firm?

    previous or current client   _____

    referral from previous or current   client   _____

    personal relationship   _____

    reputation   _____

    referral from_____   _____

    advertising _____   _____

    other_____   _____

3. When you called my office, was the telephone answered to your satisfaction?

    yes ____   no ____

    comments:

4. Were your telephone calls returned within 24 hours?

    yes ____   no ____

5. How satisfied are you with the services were handled?

1	2	3	4	5

    very   satisfied   very
    satisfied   unsatisfied

    If unsatisfied, how could it have been handled better?

6. How could the overall quality of the services be improved?

7. Would you recommend the firm to others?

    yes ____   no ____

8. Other comments (optional):

9. Name (optional):

Each of the questions is designed to elicit specific feedback. The first question identifies specific services that you provided to the client.

Question 2 identifies why the client selected you. This information is helpful in planning future marketing activities. Questions 3 and 4 measure the level of the client's satisfaction with telephone contact. Questions 5 through 7 are intended to measure the client's overall satisfaction with the your service. If completed, question 9 will enable you to undertake damage control activities with unhappy clients. If the questionnaire indicates that a named client is very unhappy about some aspect of your service, you should investigate the concern and follow up with the client. This will enable you to prevent a similar problem from arising in the future. You can also assure the client that his or her opinions are important to you.

The best format for questionnaires is a single letter sized form, printed on one side only. Such a questionnaire is more likely to be completed and returned than a longer one. You should send a covering letter, thanking the client for having chosen the firm, explaining the reason for the questionnaire, and requesting that the questionnaire be completed and returned as soon as possible. To increase the response rate, the questionnaire should be a separate mailing, i.e. it should not be included with another mailing. It should also include a self addressed stamped or postage paid envelope. If you have advertising specialties such as pens, pencils, key chains etc. with your name on them, you should include one for your client as a thank you for his or her cooperation in the survey.

Except for the comments, which invite open ended responses, the questionnaire lends itself to computer assisted analysis.

As well as measuring client satisfaction on completion of specific work, it is helpful to conduct general client satisfaction surveys from time to time. The benefits of these surveys will be maximized if samples of your client base are surveyed.

The survey should include satisfied as well as less-than-satisfied clients. To ensure a representative sample, respondents should be selected at random from the following groups to avoid bias:

- type of client: individual, institutional etc.
- size of client, by sales or employees
- clients from different practice areas
- frequent and less frequent users
- clients from different time periods.

It is important that questionnaire respondents include individuals who make the decisions as well as your client contacts. Ultimately, it is the decision makers who must be satisfied; it is to be hoped that their satisfaction is based on the actual users' satisfaction.

Provided the sample is truly representative of your overall client base, the results of the survey should reflect your total client base.

Figure 17-3 is a sample of a questionnaire that could be adapted for use in measuring the general satisfaction of individual clients.

Figure 17-3
Client Service Questionnaire
(for individuals)

I am committed to constantly improving the quality of my services to clients. Feedback from clients is an important component of this process.

I would appreciate your taking a few minutes to complete this brief questionnaire to provide me with your feedback. Please feel free to add appropriate comments.

1. Professional services provided _____ .

2. When you call my office, is the telephone answered to your satisfaction?

    yes _____   no _____

    comments:

3. Are your telephone calls returned within 24 hours?

    yes _____   no _____

    comments:

4. How satisfied are you with how the services were handled?

    1   2   3   4   5
    |----------------|----------------|----------------|----------------|
    very   satisfied   very
    satisfied   unsatisfied

    If unsatisfied, how could the services been handled better?

5. Please rate the overall quality of the services.

    Excellent   _____
    Very Good   _____
    Good   _____
    Fair   _____
    Poor   _____

6. How could the overall quality of the services be improved?

7. Would you recommend our firm to others?

    yes _____   no _____

    If so why?
    If not why not?

8. Other comments (optional):

9. Name (optional):

Questions 3 through 6 are intended to measure the clients' overall satisfaction with the firm's service. Similarly, if completed, question 9 will enable you to undertake damage control activities if necessary.

Figure 17-4 is a sample questionnaire that could be used for conducting a quality service survey of business clients. This format could be adapted for government and institutional clients.

Figure 17-4
Quality Service Questionnaire
(for business clients)

	strongly agree				strongly disagree
1. You provide the level of services that we expect.	1	2	3	4	5
comments or suggestions for improvements:					
2. You keep us informed of business and regulatory changes on a timely and proactive basis	1	2	3	4	5
comments or suggestions for improvements:					
3. Your firm understands our business and the industry in which we operate	1	2	3	4	5
comments or suggestions for improvements:					
4. You add value to our business by providing general business advice	1	2	3	4	5
comments or suggestions for improvements:					
5. You complete various assignments on a timely basis, meet agreed upon deadlines and respond quickly to questions and other requests.	1	2	3	4	5
comments or suggestions for improvements:					
6. You return phone calls promptly.	1	2	3	4	5
comments or suggestions for improvements:					
7. You take an innovative and aggressive approach to resolving our business problems	1	2	3	4	5
comments or suggestions for improvements:					

---

	strongly agree				strongly disagree
8. You demonstrate a genuine interest in our business	1	2	3	4	5
comments or suggestions for improvements:					
9. Your fees are fair and competitive with respect to services provided	1	2	3	4	5
comments or suggestions for improvements:					
10. Your brochures and mailings other matters are informative.	1	2	3	4	5
comments or suggestions for improvements:					
11. We would not hesitate to recommend you to other business acquaintances.	1	2	3	4	5
comments or suggestions for improvements:					
12. Our other professional advisors have positive comments about you.	1	2	3	4	5
comments or suggestions for improvements:					
13. You makes us feel that our business patronage is really appreciated.	1	2	3	4	5
comments or suggestions for improvements:					

Business Name

The format used in this sample will facilitate quick and easy responses by appropriate client representatives of business or similar clients. This format also facilitates computer assisted tabulation of the questionnaires.

Improving Client Satisfaction

Client feedback is the starting point for improving client satisfaction. Reassuring as it may be to learn that clients are generally satisfied with your service, the real purpose of the surveys described above is to identify opportunities for improving client service.

Improvement opportunities can be identified in a number of ways. Individual comments can identify specific concerns. These concerns might be isolated examples of problems in the delivery of service. If further investigation indicates that a problem exists, you should take remedial action to resolve the problem. Even if the problem is the client's perception of a problem, you should take action to address the perception.

Individual concerns could also be early indications of a growing pattern. If this is the case, corrective action should be taken.

Implementing improvements suggested by a client survey can also provide you with a vehicle for obtaining additional feedback from clients. Once improvements have been defined but not yet implemented, clients can be asked for their opinions.

For example, a client survey might indicate that a process by which information is exchanged between the firm and its clients could be improved. As a result, you have considered a number of alternative improvements, which include the increased use of fax transmissions, the use of computer modems, and the exchange of information on floppy disks. You might ask a number of clients which alternative they would prefer. This could be done by asking clients individually — in person, by phone or mail.

The measuring process provides an invaluable "feedback loop" for clients. It is this feedback loop that provides clients with the opportunity of helping you to design and deliver services that meet their unique needs and expectations.

18 YOU ARE NOT ALONE

Attractive as the idea may be, operating a business from your home involves some major challenges. One such challenge is integrating your business life with your personal life.

Integrating Your Family and Home Business

For many of us, our jobs are a central focus of our lives. Our education and training are intended to make us productive and contributing, members of society. There is much rejoicing when we obtain our first real jobs, as opposed to temporary and part-time jobs. Promotions are greeted with similar celebrations. Conversely, there is much despair when we lose our jobs. For many, the loss of a job is a form of death, with friends and relatives offering the same type of support they would had the loss been an actual death.

Our jobs give us a place to go, something to do, and people with whom to work and sometimes to socialize. This changes with the establishment of a home business. We still have a place to go, but it is not out. We still have something to do but somehow it is just not the same. There are people with whom we can socialize, but instead of colleagues, with whom we share the same work-a-day lives, these people are family members whose working lives do not include us.

Clearly, operating a home business requires adjustments to domestic life. If family members are expected to take the place of colleagues for purposes discussing work and other current affairs, this expectation should be realistic. If you and your spouse do not share the same interest in baseball and politics, you should look elsewhere for a discussion partner. Similarly, if as work-at-home spouse, you are expected to undertake family chores, like starting meals or scheduling appointments, these expectations should be discussed and agreed upon.

Other areas in which family life and work life must each be adjusted include involvement of family members in the business, general housekeeping around designated office space, personal use of business equipment such as computer and telephone etc. by family members and entertaining guests during business hours. All of these issues can be easily resolved. The resolution does, however, require ongoing discussion and learning by experience.

Fighting Isolation

Another challenge is fighting isolation. The reality is that you will be working alone for considerable periods of time. You won't have colleagues and associates readily available to discuss work related issues, help with decision-making or even go for coffee or discuss the latest sports or political events. Running a business from home can be very lonely.

This sense of loneliness can also be experienced as you provide services to your clients. Although you may have chosen to limit your services to a narrow range, situations will arise in which your clients will look to you for more services than you can realistically deliver. You may know what has to be done but lack either or both the personal know-how or the network contacts to provide the additional services.

Administrative and management concerns can also seem overwhelming, especially if you lack relevant experience. Bookkeeping, mass mailings and a broad range of similar tasks can appear as insurmountable obstacles for one individual operating his or her home business.

However, you need not work alone or in total isolation unless you choose to. There are ways of exchanging ideas and resources with others. Work gets done because people know and help other people.

If an individual can help you, he or she will probably do so. In business as in other areas of life, it is usually necessary to ask for what you need. The following groups of individuals outline possible sources of help.

Including Family, Friends and Neighbours

Remember that your family includes your immediate family — spouse and children — and your extended family — parents, siblings, aunts, uncles, cousins and so on. Your immediate family should be your primary source of moral and emotional support as you develop your business. They are the ones who will help you over the many crises, large and small, that you will encounter. They will cheer your achievements and rejoice in your ultimate success. They can also provide invaluable assistance in all aspects of your business. My wife, for example has played a very active role in the development of this book. One daughter continues to assist with mass mailings and administrative tasks.

Your extended family will know people that you don't. This means that they might be able to refer you to specific resources — money, skills, expertise, knowledge etc. — to which you might have otherwise not known about.

Friends and neighbours can play a similar but more objective role. They too can provide the moral support that you need when you sense that you have the entire weight of the world resting on your shoulders. They also may be able to refer you to resources that you might need.

Involving Former Colleagues and Associates

As most large organizations continue to cut back and downsize, many of your former colleagues and associates are doing the same thing that you are: running their own business from home. This means that many of the services that were formerly available only from large organizations at a high cost are now readily accessible to you at affordable rates. This represents a growing source of client service and management help for you.

Your newly independent former colleagues and associates can help you in three major ways. First, for a pre-arranged referral fee, you can refer client work directly to people, extending the range of services that you provide to your clients. Second, they can work with you in serving your clients, with their fees incorporated into your account. This will also extend your range of client services. Third, if they are unable to assist you directly, they will probably be able to refer you to others who can help you.

Don't be prepared to write off your former colleagues and associates who are still working with larger organizations. They and their business organization might be hungry for work. As a result, they might be very receptive to helping you to serve your client for reduced fees. You won't know if you don't ask. Further, since they may be concerned about their own future with their organization, they probably maintain contact with others like you who have started their own home businesses. This enables them to refer you to others who might have the resources that you require.

It is prudent to maintain contact and good relationships with your former colleagues and associates. As well as being a source of referrals to necessary resources, these individuals could also refer business to you. Make sure that the relationship goes both ways. Just as these individuals can help you, you should be prepared to assist them in any way that you can. This will help to increase the effectiveness of your referral network.

Joining Professional, Trade and Business Associations

There are thousands of professional, trade and business associations in North America. These organizations exist for one or both of two main reasons: to promote the interests of their members and to provide services to their members. Services could include training and continuing education, publications and networking opportunities.

To extend your network contacts, you should join one or more of those associations, preferably those whose members provide services similar to yours. This will provide access to a broad range of resources that will help you serve your clients better.

There are also many organizations that provide services to home businesses. Membership will help you to operate your own business more effectively. Appendix B contains a partial listing of such associations. If you know of any organization that is not listed but should be, please let me know so that I can add it to future editions.

In addition to association publications, there is a great deal of other material published for business in general and home businesses in particular. This material will yield a wealth of useful information. A selection of this material is included in Appendix C.

Drawing on Suppliers' Resources

If asked, your suppliers can help you tremendously. Your suppliers include all of those people who provide you with goods and services: your accountant, lawyer and banker, your marketing and advertising consultants, your office outfitter, your printer etc. As well as providing you with specific goods and services they can provide such information as insights into how other businesses like yours have handled specific issues, details of new developments or new service opportunities that might be worth considering. Being active in the business community, they will also be in a position to refer you to potential clients and to refer potential clients to you.

There are many other "hidden" suppliers who have great potential to help you. These are the people that you don't know about but who can do something significant for you. This could include the neighbour down the street who used be the bookkeeper in a large business and would now like to do some bookkeeping from her home. What about the former secretary who would like to do some wordprocessing or secretarial work at home using her own computer or word processor? When I was having trouble with a new printer, I asked for help from a neighbour, whom I knew to be an engineer and very interested in computers. Not only was the problem quickly resolved, we reinforced the good neighbour policy on our street. With their high level of computer literacy many students make excellent part time employees. There is considerable help available from these and similar "hidden" suppliers. All that you have to do is to discover it and ask for it. You will be pleasantly surprised at the results.

These suggestions include only some of the possible sources of help as you develop and operate your home business. Your own resources and contacts can extend this list considerably. In seeking outside help, remember that help is available — you just have to ask for it and be willing and able to reciprocate in some way.

19 JUST DOING IT

As you develop and build your home business you are likely to be successful if you try to follow these ten commandments and avoid the deadly sins.

The Ten Commandments Of Running Your Home Business

1 Maintain Steady Business Hours

Although you are physically separated from the business community, your home business operation must be accessible to and compatible with it. This means operating your business during hours compatible with those of your existing clients, potential clients, contacts and referral sources.

Further, by maintaining steady business hours, you will develop the discipline of concentrating on your work responsibilities, minimizing potential impact from household distractions. Equally important, you will minimize the spillover of business activities into family and social life.

2 Maintain A Separate Business Telephone Line

A separate business telephone line will make it easier for clients to contact you. The separate line will be listed in the telephone directory and Yellow Pages if you choose. With a separate business line, all business calls will be handled in a professional and businesslike manner.

The separate line will also make it possible to close

shop when you are no longer working. An answering machine or answering service will ensure that business calls are answered appropriately after normal business hours.

3 Establish Your Office Away From Living Areas

As much as possible, your business activities should be separated from your personal activities. This will ensure that client paperwork does not get used for grocery lists or other family notes and messages. The physical separation will also help protect the confidentiality of your dealings with clients.

Having your office away from living areas will also help you maintain the personal discipline that you need to work at home. Some people go so far as to physically leave the house when it is time to go to work. They then walk around the block, re-enter the house (often by a different door than the one they went out) and proceed to the office.

4 Organize Your Office Efficiently

Unless your office is located in a very unusual setting, you can expect few clients to physically come to it (One consultant, who for a short time operated his business from his sail boat moored in a local marina reports that while located there, every one of his clients came to see him.) As a result of not having to maintain appearances for visitors, there is a risk of your home office becoming an unmanageable jungle of paper, books and other flotsam and jetsam of office life.

You should organize and maintain your home office according to the same standards that you would use in standard office premises. As well as helping to reinforce your personal discipline, efficient organization will prevent important pieces of paper from going astray.

5 Establish and Follow Definite Work Routines

Your home office work routines should not be significantly different from those that you followed in other work situations. All that should be different is the physical location of your office.

When you arrive in your office, regardless of whether you took the direct route or the round-about route described above, you should proceed with your normal work routine. This will involve planning your day and working according to plan.

6 Use Fixed Price Contracts

Prices for your services should be a set contract price based on the value that your clients will receive; i.e. a set fee rather than hourly or daily rates.

7 Sell Value

Clients are primarily interested in what they will be receiving for their money; they are less interested in either the time you spend on a project or what your rates are. Paying for your services on a fixed price basis, clients can attach a cost to the benefits that they will receive.

8 Follow Your Business Plan and Your Marketing Plan

Once completed, these plans represent a significant investment of time and energy. They are not intended to be historical documents, cast in stone and bound for the archives. They should serve as road-maps or blue prints, providing you with an overall sense of direction. These plans will help you to remember that when you are up to your backside in allegators, your overall objective is to drain the swamp. They should give you the inspiration and direction to keep forging ahead to your goals when you seem to be bogged down in details.

For future reference, you should record any changes or modifications to your business or marketing plan. This will help ensure the accuracy of your planning process the next time you go through it. It will also help ensure that your goals and strategies are realistic in light of you, your services and your clients.

9 Extend Your Services Through Sub-Contracts, Joint Ventures and Part-time Staff

With limited resources, there are limits to the services that you can provide directly and to the number and type of clients that you can serve. By subcontracting services to others, or working on projects as a joint venture, you can dramatically increase your service potential.

Similarly, by hiring part time support staff, as needed, you can also significantly increase your service capability. The same principles apply: know what you need and ask for it.

10 Stand Behind Your Services

Your services are at the very least as good as those of your competitors. If this were not true, you would not have started your business in the first place. Your commitment to providing top quality services to your clients should be high enough that you can guarantee your clients' satisfaction. This is not "satisfaction guaranteed or money refunded." The guarantee is "satisfaction guaranteed or I'll do whatever it takes to make you happy". Note also that you are guaranteeing your services, not the end results. You can guarantee your services because you can control them; you can't guarantee end results because you cannot guarantee your clients' actions. Ensure that you and your client understand the distinction.

The Seven Deadly Sins Of Running Your Home Business

1 Allowing Personal Interruptions During Business Hours

There is no perfect working environment. In traditional office settings, interruptions come in the form of telephone calls, unscheduled visitors, co-workers and supervisors shifting your priorities and support staff seeking direction and instructions.

The potential for interruptions is equally high in the home office. On your residence telephone line, you will be subjected to unsolicited telemarketing and sundry personal or family related calls. Neighbours may drop by for a chat; family members might leave you with a list of chores and errands. The list of potential interruptions goes on.

To minimize these interruptions, you can stop answering the residence telephone, or at least use an answering machine during your working hours. After all, if you were working away from the home, it would not be answered either. Similarly, if you, and your noisy dog if you have one, can stand not knowing who is pounding on your door and why, don't answer the door. Like the telephone, it would not be answered if you were not around.

Remind everyone, including yourself, that you are home to work, not to perform chores and errands for yourself or others.

2 Allowing Yourself To Be Distracted

Frequently, when people find out that I work at home they tell me how they couldn't do it because they would be distracted by the fridge, the TV, the VCR, the bed, the swimming pool, the garden or whatever. Like me, you will wish that they didn't do this. As long as I do not allow myself to think about all of the possible distractions, they simply do not exist for me. However, when some one mentions how they would be distracted by the fridge, I almost hear my name. Similarly when someone suggests that he would be distracted by his bed, I become very tired and simply must have a nap.

Apart from firming up your personal discipline, there are no guaranteed techniques to prevent you from becoming distracted. You might try rewarding yourself with a trip to the fridge or a nap after you have achieved specific work objectives. You might also try going for a walk or performing some exercises if you feel overcome by distractions. Ideally, you should be less distractible after your reward or diversion.

You might also schedule some work-related activities away from your home office at regular intervals. This should give you the break that you need and provide for increased concentration.

3 Working On One Project At A Time

You are likely to be more easily distracted if you work on only one project at a time. With a number of projects active at any given time, you can minimize distractions by moving from one to another. Make sure that you have one project at an appropriate break point before you move on the next. Otherwise you will waste too much time trying to remember where your were and what you had to do next.

4 Allowing Yourself To Be Seduced Into Working All The Time

For workaholics, home offices are deadly traps. It is simply too easy to slip into the office for a few minutes after dinner or before going to bed. For those individuals who work to escape or to hide from other responsibilities a home office is too convenient a hiding place.

Unless absolutely necessary, do not go back to your office after normal business hours. If you have a small piece of work to finish, or are facing a major deadline, by all means put in the extra time. Work late, start early or do whatever you would normally do in a traditional office setting. Once the project is finished, take lieu time instead of overtime and get away from the office. Do not get into the practice of going into the office after business hours just because it is convenient to do so.

5 Discounting Your Rates

Good clients, i.e. those clients that keep coming back and paying their bills, expect quality service not low prices. By discounting your rates, you are giving your clients the message that the value of your services is lower because you work at home. You don't believe this; why should you give this message to your clients?

By following commandments 6 and 7, you can present your fees in such a manner that your clients believe they are receiving lower fees because of your lower overhead. Let your clients draw their own conclusions; under no circumstances should you allow them to believe that your services are worth less because you work at home.

6 Marketing Sporadically

Although a risk for all marketing activities this is especially perilous for home businesses. Being physically removed from the business mainstream, it is often difficult to get out of the house to maintain contact with clients and potential clients. Marketing is probably easier if you can physically see members of your target market on a regular basis. As outlined earlier, marketing is an ongoing activity. You must market on a frequent basis. To do otherwise is to risk isolation from your market. Once isolated, you will have to work twice as hard to maintain your position in the marketplace.

7 Working So Much For Your Clients That You Do Not Work On Your Own Business

In its extreme form, this is the case of the cobbler's children who didn't have any shoes. The key to running any successful business — outside the home or home based —

is to give top priority to clients. It is also important to remember that your own business is a client of yours. It has needs and expectations that must be met to survive. Providing the fastest and the best client service means little if your own business is falling in on itself.

Where to From Here?

At this point, little more need be said about operating a home business. The concepts must now be applied: it is time to put the windsurfer into the water, or forget about it all together.

If you decide not to start a home business, don't despair. There are other opportunities that might be better for you. You can start this process with Richard Bolles' excellent book *What Color Is Your Parachute?* listed in Appendix C.

The ideas presented above can be of great assistance in running a home business. The responsibility for implementing them, however, rests with you; no one else can do it for you. If you are going to operate a home business, get on with it. The sooner you start, the sooner you will receive the benefits.

FOOTNOTES

1. Rowan, Roy. *The Intuitive Manager*, (New York, N.Y.: Berkley Books) p.17.

2. Faith Popcorn, *The Popcorn Report*, (New York: Doubleday, 1991)

3. Tachi Sakaiya, *The Knowledge Value Revolution or A History of the Future*, (New York: Kodansha America Inc., 1991)

4. Popcorn, p. 27

5. Popcorn, p. 43

6. Popcorn, p. 50

7. op cit at p. 69

8. Sakaiya, p. 42

9. Sakaiya, p. 53

10. See *Entrepreneur Magazine*, September, 1992

11. Ernest C. Huge, *Total Quality: An Executive's Guide for the 1990s* (Homewood, Ill: Dow Jones Irwin, 1990) pp 3-5

APPENDIX A

NOW YOU TELL ME...

I ... ABOUT YOUR HOME BUSINESS

This book was written to help you succeed in your home business.

If you currently operate a home business, I would like to know how you are doing. I would like to know what has made your business successful so I can incorporate these factors into my own operation and advise others.

Just because we learn from our mistakes, we don't all have to make the same ones. What would you advise home business people to avoid?

Please take a few minutes and describe your home business using the following guidelines. Mail or fax your response to the address listed below.

- what product or service do you provide?
- to whom do you provide this product or service?
- what secrets of success would you give to some one starting his or her own home business?
- what pitfalls or traps should be avoided? how?
- if you had to start your business all over again, what would you do differently?

To assist all home business people, I will gather this information and publish it in some form. When and where appropriate, I will use actual case examples, with the prior approval of the people involved. If I use your business as an example, I will send you a complementary copy of the publication in which your business is featured. To make this possible, please include your name and address with your responses.

Mail or fax your response to: **Home Business Press**
281 Poyntz Avenue
Willowdale, Ontario
Canada M2N 1J8

Fax: (416) 250-8637

As discussed in Chapter 17, client feedback is vital to the success of a business venture. This is true of all business ventures, including the writing and publication of this book.

Subject to readers' interest, I anticipate publishing subsequent editions. I would like you to tell me how I can improve future editions and how I can make them more helpful for people like you.

Please complete the following brief semi-formal evaluation and send it to me by mail or fax. The easiest approach would be to photocopy this page, complete the photocopy and mail or fax it back to me at the address listed in Part I.

I appreciate your co-operation.

Larry Easto

1. What did you like best about the book?

2. What content should be added to make the book more relevant to you and your situation?

3. What content should be changed to make the book more relevant to you and your situation?

4. How can the inside design and layout be improved?

5. What general comments and observations do you have?

APPENDIX B

Business Associations

The current interest in Home Business has spawned a great variety of national, regional and local networks and associations.

If you see yourself as an independent business person, reluctant to join formal organizations, feel free to skip the remainder of this Appendix. Success in your home business does not depend upon your joining associations or networks. Through your own initiatives and contacts you can obtain most of the benefits of association membership.

If on the other hand you like to join organizations and be on mailing lists, the following list will be a good starting point for you. Through the contacts that you make in these organizations, you will learn of many other groups that you can join, increasing your opportunities to extend your network of personal contacts.

AMERICAN FEDERATION OF SMALL BUSINESS
407 South Dearborn St.
Chicago IL
60605-1115
phone: (312) 427-0207

AMERICAN HOME BUSINESS ASSOCIATION
P.O. Box 995
Darien CT
06820-0995
phone: (203) 655-4380

ASSOCIATION OF HOME BUSINESS
4475 SW Scholls Ferry Road
Portland OR
97225
phone: (503) 292-9201

CANADIAN ASSOCIATION OF HOME BUSINESS
1200 East Prince of Wales Drive
Ottawa, Ontario
K2C 1M9
phone: (613) 723-7233

CANADIAN FEDERATION OF INDEPENDENT BUSINESS
401-4141 Yonge St.
Toronto, Ontario
M2P 2A6
phone: (416) 222-8022

NATIONAL SMALL BUSINESS UNITED
Suite 710
1155 15th St. NW
Washington DC
20005
phone: (202) 293-8830

NATIONAL FEDERATION OF INDEPENDENT BUSINESS
150 W 20th Ave
San Mateo CA
94403
phone: (415) 341-7441

APPENDIX C
Suggestions for Further Reading

In preparing a list of books and publications for further reading, the temptation exists to add every book or publication that in any way relates to the topic of home business, regardless of quality, date of publication or relevance. However, in recognition of the fact that most successful business people do not have great amounts of time available for further reading, the following list has been kept to a bare minimum. When applicable, books with bibliographies have been noted.

PART I: BOOKS

Bolles, Richard N. *The 1993 What Color is Your Parachute? A Practical Manual for Job-Hunters and Career Changers.* Berkley, CA: Ten Speed Press, 1992.

This is the best single source of job hunting help. If running your own business is not your cup of tea, you should definitely use this book as your guide to job hunting.

Levinson, Jay Conrad. *Guerrilla Marketing: Secrets for making big profits from Your Small Business.* Boston, MA: Houghton Mifflin Company,1984.

A beginner's guide to marketing. Provides many innovative suggestions for small business marketing activities.

Naisbitt, John and Patricia Aburdene. *Megatrends 2000 Ten New Directions for the 1990s.* New York, NY: William Morrow and Company Inc.,1990.

A sequel to the best selling *Megatrends*, this book suggests trends that might be anticipated for the 1990s. Together with the books by Popcorn and Sakiya, this book provides glimpse of the future.

Popcorn, Faith. *The Popcorn Report.* New York, NY: Doubleday, 1991

Among other benefits, this book contains a method of checking your plans against the trends identified by Faith Popcorn. The book is a "must read" for forward looking business people. Contains extensive bibliographic references.

Rowan, Roy. *The Intuitive Manager.* Boston, MA: Little Brown & Company, 1986.

An excellent discussion of the the role of intuition in business operations.

Sakaiya, Tachi. *The Knowledge Value Revolution or A History of The Future.* New York, NY: Kodansha America Inc. 1991.

Like Megatrends 2000 and The Popcorn Report, this work can serve as a guide to the future. It contains extensive bibliograhic references.

Smith, Coralee. *How To Run Your Own Home Based Business.* Chicago, IL: VGM Career Horizons, 1990.

This is an excellent reference source: it contains 14 pages of "sources of additional information" included in which are 5 pages of book listings, 6 pages of periodicals listings and 3 pages of association listings.

Ward, G. Kingsley. *Letters of A Businessman To His Daughter.* Don Mills, Ont: Harper Collins, 1987.

———, *Letters of A Businessman To His Son.* Don Mills, Ont: Harper Collins, 1985.

Both books provide advice from a self made business man to his children on how to succeed in business and in life. Although out of print, the books are possibly available from public libraries. Great for would be entrepreneurs who do not have mentors for running their businesses.

PART II: PERIODICALS

HEAD OFFICE AT HOME
Published 4 times per year
Eliza Communications
c/o Abaco Communications Ltd.
Unit 2, 145 Royal Crest Court
Markham, Ontario, Canada
L3R 9Z4
phone: (416) 477-4349

HOME BUSINESS ADVISOR
Published 8 times per year
NextStep Publications
P.O. Box 41108
Fayetteville, NC
28309
phone: (919) 867-2128

HOME BUSINESS ADVOCATE
Published 6 times per year
The Alternate Press
195 Markville Rd.
Unionville, Ontario Canada
L3R 4V8
phone: (416) 470-7930

HOME BUSINESS LINE
Published monthly
397 Post Road
Darien CT
06820
phone: (203) 655-4380

HOME BUSINESS MONTHLY
Published bimonthly
38 Briarcliffe Road
Rochester NY
14617
phone: (716) 338-1144

NATIONAL HOME BUSINESS REPORT
Published bimonthly
Barbara Brabeck Productions
P.O. Box 2137
Naperville IL
60566
phone: (312) 971-1121

INDEX

ORDER FORM

To order additional copies of this book please photocopy this form and mail the completed order form with your cheque or money order to:

HOW TO SUCCEED IN YOUR HOME BUSINESS
C/O HOME BUSINESS PRESS
281 POYNTZ AVENUE
WILLOWDALE, ONTARIO
M2N 1J8

Indicate the number of copies ordered. For orders of more than 5, please contact the publisher.

Number of Books	Price per book	S & H	G.S.T.	Total
☐ 1	$14.95	$3.00	$1.27	$19.22
☐ 2	$13.95	$4.00	$2.23	$34.13
☐ 3	$13.50	$4.50	$3.15	$48.15
☐ 4	$12.95	$5.00	$3.98	$60.78
☐ 5	$12.50	$5.50	$4.76	$72.76

Please forward book(s) to:

Name: _____

Business Name: _____

Address: _____

City_____Postal Code_____

Business Phone: (_____) _____